"*Ego Free Leadership* chronicles the dynamic struggle of a CEO as his executive coach helps him face his ego triggers. It is unabashedly authentic, with unbridled self-evaluation and unvarnished honesty."

—NIGEL MORRIS, COFOUNDER, CAPITAL ONE

"Brandon Black and Shayne Hughes have landed on a key insight: When leaders let go of ego, they unlock their potential. The story of how they improved culture and performance at Encore Capital is packed with useful lessons for coaches and leaders alike."

—MARSHALL GOLDSMITH, EXECUTIVE COACH, BUSINESS EDUCATOR, AND *NEW YORK TIMES* BEST-SELLING AUTHOR, RANKED NUMBER ONE LEADERSHIP THINKER IN THE WORLD BY THINKERS50

"An authentic read! I partnered with LaL to lead two large-scale organizational turnarounds: first as Center Director of NASA's Langley Research Center, and then later as VP for Operations of the contractor operating the Nevada National Security Site for the Nuclear Security Administration. LaL led both my leadership teams through profoundly successful cultural transformations that produced breakthrough business results. In reading *Ego Free Leadership*, I could easily replace Brandon's name with my own. This book captures the challenges—and solutions—of leading large scale change."

—ROY BRIDGES, AIR FORCE MAJOR GENERAL AND FORMER CENTER DIRECTOR, NASA KENNEDY SPACE CENTER AND NASA LANGLEY RESEARCH CENTER

"The framework presented in *Ego Free Leadership* has had a profound influence on my research and teaching over the past fifteen years. I'm thrilled to see it finally brought to life in this captivating story of one CEO and his team's transformational leadership journey. This book is a must-read for any leader who wants to make a difference."

—ROBIN ELY, PROFESSOR AND FACULTY CHAIR, GENDER INITIATIVE, HARVARD BUSINESS SCHOOL

"I'm a big admirer of the work that Shayne Hughes and the team at Learning as Leadership perform. The practices and concepts for 'going deep' in the realm of leadership development are world-class and life changing. What is really happening, inside and out, for a leader trying to create deep change in himself and his organization? And what is happening, inside and out, for the leadership coach who is trying to help him? This groundbreaking book answers those questions by bringing readers into both sides of a transformative relationship. Hughes' and Black's story is instructive, rewarding, and inspiring."

—ROBERT KEGAN, MEEHAN RESEARCH PROFESSOR OF ADULT LEARNING AND PROFESSIONAL DEVELOPMENT, HARVARD UNIVERSITY; COAUTHOR, *IMMUNITY TO CHANGE* AND *AN EVERYONE CULTURE*

"This gripping story is propelled forward by the alternating perspectives of a CEO's candid rendition of his and the company's journey and of a deeply insightful executive coach. Black and Hughes share insights and tools that helped change the company—as well as Black's life. The book immediately had me thinking of situations I am dealing with as a leader and how I might manage them (and myself!) differently."

—JEFF BRADACH, CEO, BRIDGESPAN

"Black and Hughes offer an indispensable introduction into the power of authentic, ego-free leadership and the impact this can have on creating truly inspired organizations. If you can't attend a Learning as Leadership course or get Shayne as an executive coach, this book is the next best thing!"

—LEE RIVAS, PRESIDENT, ELSEVIER AND LEXISNEXIS HEALTH

"*Ego Free Leadership* provides a blueprint for transforming you and your organization. Filled with practical, real-life examples, the authors walk you through a process that surfaces the pain points leaders and organizations have and provides counterintuitive ways to resolve or even transcend them. Anyone can benefit, regardless of culture or background."

—MARTIN N. DAVIDSON, JOHNSON AND HIGGINS PROFESSOR OF BUSINESS, DARDEN GRADUATE SCHOOL OF BUSINESS; AUTHOR OF THE END OF DIVERSITY AS WE KNOW IT

"Hughes and Black do an outstanding job of bringing the power of the Learning as Leadership methodology to life in this captivating and authentic account of a CEO's journey for true leadership excellence."

—STEVE MACADAM, PRESIDENT AND CEO, ENPRO INDUSTRIES

"Learning as Leadership has had a profound impact on the Edna McConnell Clark Foundation and on me personally as well as professionally. Reading Brandon Black's and Shayne Hughes' account of one CEO's experience with the program deeply resonated with my own, and I highly recommend anyone interested in building strong, resilient leadership teams to pick up this book immediately."

—NANCY ROOB, PRESIDENT AND CEO, THE EDNA MCCONNELL CLARK FOUNDATION

"Black and Hughes use real-life challenges to illustrate how the ego gets in the way of effective leadership and teamwork. *Ego Free Leadership* is an invaluable read for anyone interested in building a successful leadership team or organization."

—KEVIN PEARSON, VICE-CHAIRMAN, M&T BANK

"This book is an engaging and entertaining read, and much more. It reveals wise and powerful insights about how, despite our best intentions, we can be the biggest obstacles to our own success and the success of those around us."

—JENNIFER CROCKER, OHIO EMINENT SCHOLAR IN SOCIAL PSYCHOLOGY, OHIO STATE UNIVERSITY

"*Ego Free Leadership* tells a powerful story of how vulnerability brings us closer to our people, teams, and goals. Hughes and Black offer a wealth of insights to business leaders seeking growth in themselves and their organizations!"

—SKIP POTTER, CHIEF TECHNOLOGY OFFICER, NIKE

"In *Ego Free Leadership*, Black and Hughes take us through one CEO's successful, inspiring, and instructive journey towards taking responsibility for his own messes. We learn how he put his ego in the service of, rather than in the way of, creating the kind of high-performance, mutually supportive organization to which we all aspire. Damn. I wish they had written it (and I had read it) decades ago."

—MARTY LINSKY, HARVARD KENNEDY SCHOOL; COAUTHOR OF *LEADERSHIP ON THE LINE*

"Another self-absorbed CEO with a management guru—what could I possibly learn? Don't let your ego get in the way! Black, Hughes, and Encore's bumpy yet remarkable journey provides unvarnished insights and lessons for all of us as we seek personal, leadership, and business development. I benefited yesterday and I will benefit today."

—SCOTT HUENNEKENS, PRESIDENT AND CEO, VERB SURGICAL INC.

"*Ego Free Leadership* brings fresh insights into what it means to lead, how we can get in our own way, and how we might help others develop their leadership. Even more, Black and Hughes deliver specific tools for attacking our worst ego-based problems, helping us become better leaders for our teams and organizations."

—SUSAN J. ASHFORD, PROFESSOR OF MANAGEMENT AND ORGANIZA-TIONS, STEPHEN M. ROSS SCHOOL OF BUSINESS, UNIVERSITY OF MICHIGAN

"*Ego Free Leadership* tells a fascinating, real-life saga about how our ego traps us in a prison. So many of us significantly underestimate how our ego hijacks our leadership and organizations, causing us to accomplish much less than we could otherwise."

—GEORGE McCOWN, COFOUNDER AND OPERATING DIRECTOR, AMERICAN INFRASTRUCTURE FUNDS; CHAIRMAN EMERITUS, WORLD BUSINESS ACADEMY

"Organizations fail when the ego needs of its leaders hijack its mission. In this compelling, true account, the CEO of a company on the verge of failure is guided through the deep learning that saves his leadership and his enterprise. A powerful, practical story of egos tamed and an organization resurrected."

—HARRY SPENCE, FORMER COMMISSIONER, MASSACHUSETTS DEPARTMENT OF SOCIAL SERVICES; ADMINISTRATOR, MASSACHUSETTS TRIAL COURT

EGO FREE
LEADERSHIP

EGO FREE
LEADERSHIP

Ending the Unconscious Habits
That Hijack Your Business

BRANDON BLACK & SHAYNE HUGHES

GREENLEAF
BOOK GROUP PRESS

Published by Greenleaf Book Group Press
Austin, Texas
www.gbgpress.com

Distributed by Greenleaf Book Group

For ordering information or special discounts for bulk purchases, please contact Greenleaf Book Group at PO Box 91869, Austin, TX 78709, 512.891.6100.

Design and composition by Greenleaf Book Group
Cover design by Greenleaf Book Group

Cataloging-in-Publication data is available.

Print ISBN: 978-1-62634-379-5

eBook ISBN: 978-1-62634-380-1

Part of the Tree Neutral® program, which offsets the number of trees consumed in the production and printing of this book by taking proactive steps, such as planting trees in direct proportion to the number of trees used: www.treeneutral.com

TreeNeutral®

Printed in the United States of America on acid-free paper

17 18 19 20 21 22   10 9 8 7 6 5 4 3 2 1

First Edition

To Aidan, Gabriel, Jeremi, Leah, and Trevor

May you and your generation be inspired leaders of the future,
always seeking to bring out the best in others.

CONTENTS

LIST OF BOXES AND FIGURES

ENDING THE UNCONSCIOUS HABITS THAT HIJACK YOUR BUSINESS

———

BRANDON

It's January 2005, and our company is under siege: Industry turbulence has sent costs soaring, and profits are drying up before our eyes. As Encore Capital's president and COO, I help devise our response to the crisis: Hire top-caliber key executives, start a new business vertical, acquire a company outside our core business, and open an overseas call center. We'll turn this ship around; we've done it before.

I pride myself on having a highly analytical, strategic mind while still being a people person. I know how to guide groups to the right decisions. I'm Brandon Black, age thirty-seven, and thanks to good timing, great mentors, and a lot of luck, my career path has largely been one success after another. I'm expected to replace our CEO when he retires in the fall. I'm ready.

Or so I thought.

By October 2005, when I became CEO of this publicly traded financial services company (Nasdaq: ECPG), the turnaround strategies were floundering. Our new business vertical was going sideways, our acquisition was a cultural and financial misfit, and our call center in India was struggling to get off the ground. Costs of new deals in our core business kept increasing. Our stock price had dropped 30 percent in the previous twelve months. I was rattled.

The shareholders were unhappy, and the board was questioning our decisions. I turned to my executive team for results, only to find that my high-caliber new hires were struggling to understand our complex business. Strategy meetings were constrained by people fighting for airtime or dismissing each other's ideas. When I met offline with my direct reports to focus on operational issues, they made excuses and pointed fingers.

Determined to succeed, even single-handedly, I went around them—only to confront entrenched silos. Instead of sharing resources and solving problems together, department heads fought over who called the shots, hadn't delivered results, or weren't suited to do their jobs.

I initially shrugged off these personality conflicts and turf wars. *Similar dysfunctions plagued my previous employers, yet they still succeeded. Our major competitors can't be any better. A few wins and everybody will be fine.*

But market conditions worsened, and the added stress pushed us further into our self-serving corners. Morale was at an all-time low.

Grasping at anything that could give me hope, I signed my executive team up for a series of leadership development seminars. I didn't need the help, but they certainly did.

That didn't change anything. In poker, they say if you can't find the mark, you're it. In leadership, if you look around and think everyone else is the problem, it means you're the problem. That was me. I first resisted the reality that key aspects of my leadership style were having a detrimental impact on my team. Then, finally, I committed to facing it. That decision fundamentally changed the trajectory of Encore.

Three years later, the financial crisis of 2008 decimated our industry. Ninety percent of our competitors went bankrupt or shuttered their operations. Encore Capital could easily have been one of them.

We weren't.

During the greatest recession since the 1930s, Encore thrived. Between 2009 and 2013, our revenues and profits increased 300 percent, operating costs declined 30 percent, and the stock price rose 1200 percent. How did we create this miracle?

Here's what we did *not* develop:

- A unique strategy—Every industry player was bidding on the same deals and building overseas call centers.

- A hidden source of revenue—Laws and regulations for our industry made innovation nearly impossible.

- A game-changing technology—Our industry-best analytics only heightened our awareness of how dire things were.

- A mercilessly reduced cost structure—We knew asking people to do more for less wasn't going to save us.

Instead, our competitive advantage came from recognizing and stopping the specific ways in which we were working *against* each other.

This awareness allowed us to take full advantage of the disrupted marketplace and unlock *hundreds of millions of dollars per year* of enhanced performance. Our journey is what inspired my leadership coach, Shayne Hughes, and me to write this book.

Encore's transformation began when I acknowledged the destructive elements of my own ego. I learned that my need to be right, coupled with a robust fear of failure, made me defensive and argumentative; unbeknownst to me, these tendencies had far-reaching negative impacts on my colleagues and the company. When I committed to change, I gave my executive team and other leaders in the company the opportunity to openly address their own ego-driven behaviors and skill gaps. We each examined how our distrust and our judgments were fueling the internal politics and divisions we blamed others for. And we stopped it.

A new foundation of trust allowed us to take quick, decisive action on Encore's most important priorities. We collaboratively solved problems such as how to create an international collection strategy, which no one thought was possible. We prioritized resources throughout the company as needed, and without drama, focusing on the initiatives that would have the greatest benefit.

Our cultural transformation didn't happen overnight with a series of quick-fix solutions. Over the course of several years, we partnered with Shayne and Learning as Leadership to get at the root causes of our challenges—and eliminate them.

We learned a different way to lead and to support each other as we all elevated the company to unexpected levels of performance.

SHAYNE

My name is Shayne Hughes and I'm the president of Learning as Leadership. I've been an executive coach for twenty-five years, partnering with leaders to bring about culture change within their organizations. I am grateful to Brandon for sharing his story because it allows us to explore a subject I care deeply about.

The politics, power struggles, and dysfunctional behavior Brandon faced in 2005 are nearly ubiquitous in organizations of all sizes. Blaming, avoiding conflict, overcontrolling, assuming ill intent—sometimes these behaviors are so constant we stop noticing. They are the air we breathe. Stress and conflict undermine employee satisfaction and engagement. In fact, a September 2015 Gallup Poll measured nationwide employee engagement levels at 31 percent—and that's a peak for the past five years! Even more troubling, almost 20 percent of employees are actively *disengaged*.

It's all the more aggravating that the solutions to this quagmire seem so obvious. Ask any group of employees to describe an ideal team or organizational culture, and they will tell you: supportive, transparent, authentic, collaborative, trusting. But inquire about their current company's culture, and the list usually looks very different: competitive, political, territorial, untrusting, conflict averse.

If we all know the characteristics of a healthy team and organizational culture, why do egos and rivalries keep coming back? Are there ways to eliminate them? My company's founders, my colleagues, and I are passionate about exposing the destructive effects of the ego—and releasing the boundless human energy and outcomes that are possible when we shed these unnecessary tendencies.

Dysfunction is so entrenched because it occurs automatically, whenever a person experiences stress or fear. Although unproductive reactions seem like personality traits, they are, in fact, learned, *very predictable*—and completely changeable. In understanding how anxiety about your value, competence, and well-being can hijack your behavior, you will discover the time-tested strategies that Encore employed to forge a healthy, creative, and high-performing organization.

Note, however, that we don't present any silver bullets in *Ego Free Leadership*. That's what Brandon initially wanted when he became Encore's CEO, and his efforts to hold his team accountable to more functional behaviors went in vain. Like most smart, self-aware, and highly successful executives, *Brandon underestimated how his own ego-driven dysfunctions created a team and organizational culture that virtually guaranteed broader dysfunction.*

Are you willing to look at this for yourself?

In the coming pages, Brandon will share his journey. You'll understand his fears and his team's challenges, and you'll watch him break through his limitations as a leader. He'll take the risk of revealing what we all think and feel but usually don't admit—sometimes, not even to ourselves. He'll take you on a wild ride, and together, he and I will help you understand the connection between individual leadership obstructions, cultural dysfunction, and business results.

Encore Capital collects distressed consumer debt. It isn't a glamorous job, but if no one does it, America's financial system grinds to a halt. *How* it is done, however, makes an invaluable difference in the lives of both consumers and employees. Encore's management team embraced that opportunity despite external skepticism about their motives. They created a culture in which imperfection, empathy, and growth were valued. They sought to heal rifts across departments, cultures, and genders. They encouraged people to care about the plight of their consumers.

In the process, they discovered that the upside business value of decreasing ego within an organization is not incremental, but exponential. It's the difference between 300 percent growth and bankruptcy.

CHAPTER 1

THAT VOICE IN YOUR HEAD DOES MORE DAMAGE THAN YOU REALIZE

———

Our Preoccupation with Self-Worth

BRANDON

I stepped into the blazing August 2005 sunshine of New York City. The temperature was 95 degrees and the humidity hit me like a wave. I was headed to the biggest meeting of my career and had decided to clear my head by walking the ten blocks from my hotel. After a dozen paces, however, I was soaked in sweat.

My boss, Carl Gregory, was retiring as the CEO of Encore Capital Group, and the board of directors had agreed to make me his successor. I was fortunate to achieve a lot of success early in my career: I was managing thousands of people by the time I was twenty-seven, had helped Encore avoid bankruptcy, and was on the Nasdaq stage when we took the company public in 2003. Now, at thirty-seven, I was poised to be its leader. I was on my way to finalize the terms of my agreement with Nelson Peltz, a member of the board and Encore's largest shareholder. I had worked at Encore for five years, and Nelson and I had a good relationship. He had a reputation for being a ruthless negotiator, though, and several board members offered to advise me on how to handle the meeting. Instead, I did my own homework, even hiring a compensation consultant to benchmark my proposal. My request was fair and well deserved. I was confident I would prevail.

I arrived a few minutes before our scheduled start time of 2:30 pm, which gave me time to wipe the sweat off my face. We were meeting in a restaurant partially owned by Nelson. It was between the lunch and dinner service, and when we sat down, we were the only two people in the place. I laid out my rationale in fine detail.

"Well done, Brandon," Nelson said when I finished. "But this is a zero-sum game. Every dollar I pay you is a dollar that doesn't go to the shareholders. As the largest shareholder, I don't like that."

"I understand," I replied, "but a dollar means a lot more to me than it does to you."

"No," he said flatly, "a dollar is a dollar."

I couldn't believe his response. I made my arguments again, this time with added emphasis on the salary benchmarking, which was clearly impartial. He didn't budge and told me that his offer was final. Time to walk out or fold. I stood up, looked at the door—and then shook his hand. Nelson knew all along that there was no way I was going to walk away from this opportunity. He had all the leverage. Never take a knife to a gunfight.

I prided myself on my ability to convince others. I had often been the young executive having to overcome perceptions that I wasn't up to the challenge. Winning this negotiation was my chance to prove I could roll with the big guys. I couldn't believe how poorly it went. I got the job, but it still felt like I belonged at the kids' table.

The air outside was stifling, the heat and humidity mixing with my anger and embarrassment. I felt naive and inexperienced. I was supposed to meet another board member, Alex, for a drink. He had offered to help me negotiate with Nelson, but I refused. As I walked, I racked my brain for any plausible excuse to cancel.

The room at Smith and Wollensky's was crowded. Alex was at the bar and he waved me over. He raised his glass and toasted my success. I should have been thrilled. Instead, it felt like I had blown my first big opportunity. Should I have held out for more money? If I couldn't advocate for myself, was I really up to this job? I tried to shove my doubts away on the flight home to San Diego. Dana, my wife of just a few weeks, met me at the airport. We went through the details of the meeting, and she was relieved I hadn't tested Nelson's resolve.

Over the weekend we talked about how I planned on handling the challenges facing Encore. It was a period of unprecedented change on all fronts.

Our core business was under tremendous pressure. While the financial crisis of 2008 was still three years away, our industry had begun its own recession. Encore Capital acquires unpaid consumer debts, mainly credit cards, from banks and other large financial institutions. The company becomes the de facto creditor, and we work to collect money from those consumers who regain their ability to pay. On average, 80 percent of the consumer accounts we acquire pay us nothing. The other

20 percent pay us approximately sixty-six cents on the dollar. The critical variables that determine our profitability are the purchase price for portfolios of unpaid debt, the total dollars we collect, and the operating costs required to generate those collections. Between December 2004 and January 2005, the prices for portfolios increased by almost 100 percent, making new investments largely unprofitable. Prior years of very profitable investments had given us a small window of time to adjust our operating model. It was up to me to figure out how to adapt.

We hadn't anticipated such a dramatic shift and had no contingency plans. So, during the first eight months of 2005, we reacted by launching a variety of strategic initiatives designed to offset the price increases and diversify our revenue. Sort of like throwing spaghetti against the wall. We acquired the largest portfolio of unpaid receivables in the company's history, along with an operating site of 200 people; hired an experienced management team to create a new business vertical focused on a different asset class; acquired a company outside our core business; and opened our first international site in India. Bold moves for a company our size. The big question was whether my newly formed executive team had the leadership and business skills to make the moves pay off.

During the prior five years, as COO, I had worked closely with Carl and the company's CFO, Barry Barkley. It took time to build our leadership rapport, but the three of us found a solid working rhythm. I learned invaluable lessons from both of them. Now that era was ending.

Barry had retired in June, and Carl was stepping away in October. The new CFO, Paul Grinberg, had a world of experience and was one of the smartest people I'd ever met. But the two of us approached problems very differently. He came up with all the reasons why initiatives wouldn't work, while I could only see the finish line. I couldn't figure him out. Weren't we supposed to identify ways to grow the company? Why was he always so negative? If we were going to navigate our way through these challenging times, our relationship had to work, but we weren't clicking.

Paul wasn't the only new member on the leadership team. We had hired an Operations executive to replace me and added two leaders to oversee our new business ventures. All three were experienced, but new to our industry. I saw early on that they were struggling, but I needed to concentrate on my transition. They'd have to figure it out on their own.

As I talked this over with Dana, she was concerned that I wasn't being honest with myself. She thought I was overcommitted and wasn't organized enough to take care of all my new responsibilities. I told her I was perfectly capable of handling everything—and suggested she "focus on herself" instead.

"Now you're dismissing my feelings," she told me straight up.

From the beginning of our relationship, Dana refused to put up with my bullshit. Given that both of us were previously married, she insisted that we meet with a therapist to ensure we built a strong foundation for our relationship. She was always pushing me to be more authentic with her and with my six-year old son, Trevor. I trusted her advice when it came to our family, but I was a different person at work.

"It'll be fine," I said, hoping to end the conversation. "I just need time to focus and work with the team. We'll get there."

"Really? I've heard that before. I think you should get some help."

I nodded but didn't respond. The job would be a challenge, but I was confident. I needed to learn more about managing balance sheets and dealing with shareholders, analysts, and regulators. But my leadership capabilities were strong. I'd been successful so far, right? Besides, my team needed to see I was in control and had the answers.

I was glad to get back in the office on Monday to focus on our key initiatives. Late morning, I had a meeting with Paul to talk about our acquisition.

"We'll close on time," he said, "but I don't know how we'll fit culturally. It can be hard for founders to take direction. Getting their management team to operate with our rigor is going to be difficult. When I tried to talk to them about metrics, they kept telling me not to worry, that they knew their business."

"Do I need to fly there?" I asked.

"I'd say 'yes,' but there are too many issues here."

"What are you talking about?"

"It seems like all I do is listen to people complain about project delays and who's to blame for missed projections. The new guy, Dave, doesn't understand our business. I was babysitting while you were gone the last couple of weeks."

"OK, I can fix that."

"While you're at it, can you deal with the Technology team? They keep fighting with Operations about why critical software enhancements are more than sixty days behind schedule. When we get in a room, IT blames Operations for constantly changing the scope of the project, while the Ops guys see the IT team as rigid and incompetent." He sighed. "I've got five more examples like that."

Paul could be a glass-half-empty guy, but this time I sensed real frustration. When I had tried to address similar concerns with the executive team several weeks prior, I got polite pushback and silence. Apparently, they still hadn't gotten the message. We were in a tough spot, and this team didn't seem to have the skills or maturity to understand the magnitude of the problem. Maybe Dana was right; they did need help. I asked Paul if he had any ideas.

"I've got a solution, but it's unorthodox," he said. "The focus is on identifying unproductive leadership behaviors and involves several week-long training sessions over a year. The organization is called Learning as

Leadership, and the seminars are held in Sausalito, California. Instead of them coming here, we go to them."

I looked at him incredulously.

"It would be our team mixed with leaders from around the country," he continued hurriedly. "We get the benefit of their experience. I've done it before. It's amazing."

Where is this guy coming from? I wanted some quick help, not a multi-week distraction. Paul was so enthusiastic, though, that I didn't know how to politely turn him down. We asked two of Learning as Leadership's (LaL's) partners, Shayne Hughes and Lara Nuer, to meet with us in October, the same month I would formally become CEO. I would play along so Paul would feel like I was being a good "partner."

Shayne and Lara spent the first half of their visit meeting one-on-one with my team to get a sense of our overall challenges. When I finally stepped into the conference room to be debriefed, I was prepared for them to be arrogant, self-absorbed, and overeducated. But they neither looked nor acted like consultants I had met before. My misgivings quickly began to fade once the discussion began.

Both seemed keenly interested in understanding my challenges. Lara asked penetrating questions: "What are your developmental areas as an incoming CEO? What is the impact of your team's dysfunctions on your business performance? What do you envision would be possible if you and your team could talk openly and constructively about difficult topics?" Several leaders on my team seemed incapable of "looking in the mirror," and Lara's questions were good ones for them to address.

Shayne and Lara explained how the LaL process explores the formative experiences we've had growing up, shaping our view of the world. In particular, the process investigates how our "ego" triggers counterproductive leadership behaviors that impede performance. That certainly rang true when I looked at my team—"childish" was how I thought of some of their behavior.

While they had thoughtful answers to my questions, I still couldn't get over the time commitment and format. "It sounds like one big networking event where we commiserate and waste time on other people's problems. Why would we ever do that?" *Let's see how they respond to that.*

"You told us not five minutes ago about an executive on your team who won't acknowledge his limitations during performance reviews," Shayne responded. "You think if we come down here and make him come clean in front of the team, he's going to respond productively? In a larger group, while interacting with leaders from different industries with similar problems, he'll have the anonymity to be honest with himself. His coach will challenge him offline. Then, when he's ready, we'll talk as a team. You won't waste time, you'll save time."

"I get it," I told him. "I was just testing you."

Shayne opened his mouth, closed it, and shook his head.

I needed to buy some time to reflect on the meeting. What started out as a courtesy discussion had turned into something for me to seriously consider.

"Let me talk with Paul and think about it over the weekend," I told them. "We'll get back to you."

I knew Paul was in favor, so that was the easy part. As much as I found the travel and the comingling with others to be odd at best, Shayne and Lara's logic was compelling. But could I really commit the team to the travel and time out of the office? I kept coming back to one indisputable point: I needed a leadership development solution. Nothing else we looked at seemed promising, and LaL had a seminar starting in November. I decided to give them a shot.

At our next executive staff meeting, I told my team that we would all be attending a five-day leadership seminar up in the San Francisco

Bay Area. I reinforced the messages I took away from Shayne and Lara and let the team know that Paul had attended their program previously. When I finished, I looked around the room, expecting uniform acceptance, perhaps even a round of applause.

"Why didn't we talk about this as a group?" asked one executive.

"Who decided it was mandatory?" lamented another.

"Are you kidding me?" I snapped after several more complaints. "Many of you are new to the company and are in the largest roles of your career. We're investing a lot of money so that you can be your best. Discussion closed."

I wasn't back in my office twenty minutes before one of my vice presidents knocked on the door, raising more questions about LaL. I cut him off. "How about you just worry about getting your job done?" *If you did that,* I thought, *we wouldn't need to spend money on development.*

In preparation for our first program, LaL conducted a 360-degree feedback for each of us. A few weeks later, Shayne, now my executive coach, scheduled a debrief call to go through my results. The issues didn't surprise me: I debated people, didn't solicit information from others before making decisions, and always needed to be right. *Common traits of a strong leader,* I thought. "Don't worry," I told him. "The benefits outweigh the detriments. I debate with people to find out how attached they are to their ideas. The truly committed people continue the discussion, which gets us to the right outcome. If the final answer is what I suggested in the first place, it's only a coincidence."

"There are a lot of comments here about how people are afraid to speak up," he pointed out.

"This isn't a democracy!" He was starting to bug me now. This wasn't an issue that needed to be *solved*. "Don't you agree it's the CEO's job to make the big decisions?"

There was a long pause.

"Why do you think so many people gave the same feedback if it wasn't important to them?" he asked. "Is it possible these behaviors get in the way of your team reaching its full potential? Take your debating, for example. Is it possible that it is more about you being right than what's best for Encore?"

As far as I was concerned, CEOs needed to be confident. Having a strong ego was integral to being a successful executive. I decided not to debate this with Shayne.

"Maybe," I muttered, and then changed the topic to whether my team was taking their feedback seriously.

SHAYNE

"It's not that I *want* to be right," Brandon corrected me as I tried to deliver his 360-degree feedback in October 2005. "It's that I *am* right most of the time. That's what I get paid for."

"Uh-huh." It was the fourth point in a row he rebutted. "Even if you are right," I persisted, "people feel like you 'plow over them.' They feel intimidated and belittled. What do you think is driving this?"

"Control," Brandon answered without missing a beat. "It's my way of keeping discussions on track. Very common for CEOs."

This is going to be trouble, I thought.

Brandon's 360-degree feedback detailed his strengths and weaknesses as a leader. He was viewed as intelligent, highly competent, and outgoing, and his team generally enjoyed working for him. Like every leader, however, he had several harmful behaviors that negatively impacted his colleagues and the company culture. Although he was eager for his team to "look in the mirror" and professed that he wanted to do so as well, he nevertheless had a justification for each piece of constructive criticism. For the few weaknesses he did acknowledge, he dismissed their impact. Brandon *wanted* to learn and grow, but his involuntary responses in our calls were reactive and unproductive. He believed what he was saying and didn't think he was being defensive.

Unknowingly, his conscious intentions were being derailed by automatic reactions that prevented him from responding productively. We all do this. When faced with uncomfortable feedback, for example, each of us can shut down, discredit the source, or blame others—even though we *know* we should learn from the criticism. These reactive behaviors are a symptom of our ego, or egosystem.

Let's think of ego as a *constant preoccupation with our self-worth*. While it can feel incomprehensible, it is actually a predictable system of triggers and reactions that can be mapped out. This is our "egosystem." Each one of us has beliefs and fears about our value, and they cause defensive and/or self-promotional behaviors when under stress. Whether in a meeting, a presentation, or a relationship, part of our attention—sometimes all of it—is preoccupied by our view of our self. Are we competent? Respected? Intelligent? Liked? Attractive? Included? Each of us has a set of criteria we unconsciously judge ourselves against. When we measure up, we feel pride, even superiority. When we don't, we feel uncomfortable, stressed, often afraid.

These feelings of inadequacy or imperfection *automatically* trigger knee-jerk reactions, usually in the form of fight–flight behaviors. Although they often feel "right" in the moment, these reactions have wide-ranging negative consequences.

Brandon didn't suspect his behavior—debating, judging, being sarcastic—was undermining his goals at Encore. But who would want to suggest an out-of-the-box idea if he or she would have to defend it against the smartest and most powerful guy in the room? Or to admit a weakness if it might be used later in a sarcastic put-down? Sure, there are a couple of bold-faced leaders out there who might do this, but it's rare for a team to have even one such person.

THE EGOSYSTEM

Our preoccupation with self-worth triggers reactive behaviors with the following characteristics:

- **Automatic**—They happen without our conscious awareness.

- **Deceptively destructive**—Our ego hijacks our talents and strengths to protect our worth at the expense of others and our best intentions.

- **Very predictable**—Each one of us has three or four primary ways in which we perceive a threat to our value and react to protect it.

When triggered, our ego drives us to:

- Avoid conflict
- Blame others
- Be a perfectionist
- Get angry or defensive
- Omit or hide issues
- Shut down
- Be indecisive
- Jump to conclusions
- Judge ourselves and others
- Procrastinate
- Not ask for help
- Debate/prove others wrong

Most of our egosystem's reactions have similarly negative ripple effects on our goals and relationships. If we micromanage others, they often don't feel trusted. If we get defensive or angry, they feel attacked. If we shut down or avoid conflict, they might feel judged, abandoned, and/or unsure of where they stand. Brandon's first blind spot lay in underestimating how his own dysfunctions derailed him and his team from achieving their goals.

When people become aware of their "derailers," they typically justify these behaviors as an inflexible part of their personality. "I'm just that way"; "Take the good with the bad"; "Can't teach an old dog new tricks." *But these behaviors are not genetic.* They are learned, and even though we developed them over decades, it is never too late to unlearn them. Acknowledging these dysfunctions, and tracing them back to their roots (yes, analyzing our childhood), allows us to discover our unique form of preoccupation with self-worth.

At this point you might be thinking, "Wait, I want leaders with strong egos running my organization! They take charge and drive results." Sorry, but this book aims to debunk the "ego is good" myth.

Although leaders focused on their own success appear to make high-performing individual contributors, their ego is actually causing them to *play it safe* in their own specific way. Brandon's debating and sarcasm helped him dominate discussions. This put his direct reports too much on the defensive to ever really challenge his thinking, ensuring that Brandon never felt wrong or not smart enough. Task-driven leaders can produce vast amounts of work, but in their comfort zone, somehow never finding time for what's creative or strategic. Visionary thinkers lose interest when reality doesn't appear as brilliant as their original idea. None of this is a coincidence. As we'll explore, our ego can't stand failure, incompetence, or weakness, so it avoids what is truly challenging to us.

More disruptive, a "strong ego" mentality ultimately prioritizes individual success over the team and mission. Modeled across an organization, it generates waves of distrust and infighting, inconspicuously absorbing the majority of your workforce's energy. The unproductive mindset and behaviors revealed in this book cost you dearly in both quality of work–life balance and bottom line results.

Dissolving these tendencies—individually and as a team—will unleash the natural talents, boldness, and creativity of you and your people.

What Hijacks Our Behavior

BRANDON

Ten of us from Encore showed up in Sausalito at one of the most spectacular settings I can imagine for a vacation, let alone a leadership seminar. We were in a banquet room of the Spinnaker restaurant, situated on the waterfront across from San Francisco. We were mesmerized by the fog rolling over the hills and the sailboats cruising the bay.

Seventy people from different industries and sizes and types of businesses (for-profit, nonprofit, and government) were in attendance. I looked around the room to gauge the experience of the other participants. Would they provide any valuable advice to my team? I was still frustrated by the lack of insight from LaL's 360-degree feedback. It was time for Shayne and his team to bring their "A" game. My mindset from the beginning was "I'm the client here." I had taken the risk to hire them and needed to see immediate dividends.

Unfortunately, no insights were forthcoming. Their process was time-consuming and monotonous. We spent hours filling out charts and responding to questions about our fears and reactions. By the third day, my team and I had resorted to joking about the other participants and venting about how trapped and miserable we were.

"You've got to be kidding me, Brandon," my CIO said to me one morning as we sat on the deck during a break. "You drag us up here to become better leaders and instead we spend our time analyzing what happened thirty years ago? The only reason I'm still here is you're my boss and you can fire me if I pack up and go home."

I normally would have reacted harshly to his tone, but I agreed with every word. If we hadn't paid LaL a lot of money, I would have taken the next flight back to San Diego.

My frustration was exacerbated by superficial team conversations.

I had hoped LaL would help us get the more problematic performance and leadership issues out on the table, but no one was engaging.

Finally, on the last day, we started a discussion about Encore's challenges and began brainstorming solutions. It didn't take long, however, for the excuses to start: not enough time for all the priorities, the lack of transparency from me and Paul, executives feeling like I played favorites, and so on. I was so tired of hearing them. Toward the end of the discussion, Sharon, the SVP of Human Resources, made a suggestion I thought was off base, and I countered with a flippant response. To my amazement, she became visibly upset.

"I was just kidding," I told her. "Don't be so sensitive."

I wanted to push forward with the discussion but couldn't figure out how to do so without appearing to be even more insensitive.

"That hurt, Brandon," she finally said, looking right at me.

I met her gaze, and felt my stomach turn. She was the third person in the past month to tell me my comments could be hurtful. The therapist Dana and I were seeing had suggested to me that my sarcasm was veiled anger and that "nobody is ever 100 percent kidding." I assured her I was the exception to the rule. I grew up in a household where most communication came in the form of sarcasm; we debated anything for the sake of argument, and the person with the last word won. But we were all "just kidding."

I had tremendous respect for Sharon, and it shocked me that I'd treated her that way. Other interactions from the seminar came to mind, and I began to see that my sarcastic and disparaging tone might be more destabilizing than I thought. I wondered how many people I had hurt or relationships I had harmed because of my quick tongue.

I wasn't the only one on the team guilty of this behavior, so then and there we made an agreement not to use sarcasm in the workplace. It was a hopeful end to a lousy "learning how to lead" week.

SHAYNE

Encore Capital's first seminar was a wild ride. While we racked our brains to find a way to help them put their issues on the table, they sat in the back of the room and made fun of us and the other participants. They disappeared mid-session to shop in Sausalito's boutiques and made it clear our work was a waste of time. Conveniently, the issues they had with each other stayed carefully under wraps. We were the problem.

One exchange I witnessed that week highlighted what happened when they attempted to talk about their challenges. They were discussing the skyrocketing cost pressures in their industry.

"You guys shouldn't be so gloomy," exclaimed Dave. "We collected over five million dollars last month!"

"But our models planned for six," responded Paul, the CFO, clearly wanting to move on. "Now—"

"But our team collected 30 percent more than last year," Dave insisted. "Who does that?!"

"We bought all that debt for twice as much as last year, so at a 30 percent increase, we're underwater," Brandon explained.

"It's still a great accomplishment."

"I suppose you want to give them an extra bonus?" Paul asked.

"Yes, they need encouragement," Dave said. "They're working really hard."

"Well, when we go bankrupt and start a cheerleading company, I'll put you in charge," Brandon laughed. "But for now, why don't you let us figure this part out?"

Dave opened his mouth, then closed it. The message was clear: Dave's input wasn't helpful or wanted, and Paul and Brandon thought him stupid.

"Hold on," I said, "can we talk about what just happened?"

"No," Brandon was emphatic. "It's handled, thanks."

Sarcasm carries overtones of judgment because it often masks, through mockery, conflict avoidance. Both Paul and Brandon had concluded that Dave lacked analytical skills and didn't respect his experience. They weren't addressing this with him, however, so their frustration grew. He sensed their judgment, and felt threatened by it, but was too uncomfortable to say so. Similar dynamics were at play with other team members, and these unspoken—yet loudly expressed—criticisms were toxic to team trust. And when trust is low, our fear of others' judgments intensifies. We quickly assume any weakness or shortcoming we disclose will be held against us.

Meanwhile, our egosystem is constantly monitoring our value and status. People can say, "I don't care what others think," but that is almost universally untrue. Our brains are wired to care, and trying not to is another form of ego-protection. This fear of others' judgment creates an emotional tension or mind chatter in each of us, and we expend significant time and energy trying to manage it. At LaL, we call this monitoring "desired and dreaded images." Desired images describe how we *wish to appear* or what we want others to think of us. Dreaded images are how we *do not want to appear* or how we fear being judged.

Think of desired and dreaded images as adjectives, respectively charged with the allure of acceptance and approval or the threat of rejection and disdain. Each of us has semiconsciously decided which images are most crucial to prove (desired) or defend against (dreaded) in order to preserve our sense of value. The culture we grow up in influences the primary images we take on.

To understand why desired and dreaded images are problematic, it's critical to distinguish between *being* a characteristic and *appearing* to be it. Every member of Encore's executive team was skilled, intelligent, and hardworking. Several of them also had desired images of appearing smart, competent, and under control. Disclosing to Brandon that they were struggling carried the risk of appearing incompetent, ineffective, and not smart enough to get the job done. Feeling weak or inferior bruises our egosystem's sense of self-worth, and we'll do almost anything to avoid that discomfort. Since Brandon was quick to judge, his executives' egosystems wouldn't let them take the risk of disclosure.

COMMON DESIRED AND DREADED IMAGE DUOS

- **Competent** (smart/stupid, capable/incapable, experienced/ignorant)
- **Likeable** (kind/mean, reasonable/unreasonable, humble/arrogant)
- **Ethical** (generous/selfish, honest/dishonest, a good/bad person)
- **Strong** (self-sufficient/needy, powerful/powerless, in control/helpless)

All of this helps explain why an intelligent and highly successful leader would commit his management team to a weeklong leadership development activity—only to actively undermine it and allow his team to do the same. There was too much fear about what would happen if people said what they really thought. For Encore, it was too uncomfortable to even talk about talking about it.

Leaders in every organization fall into this form of dysfunction. Our rational mind knows that we *should* talk about our difficulties, ask a question if we don't understand, or deliver that difficult message. But more primal emotions of fear and vulnerability prevail. Not acknowledging our difficulties, however, cuts us off from help or mentoring, increasing the likelihood that we'll underperform. *Trying to appear competent actually causes us to learn and grow more slowly and, over time, become less competent.* The longer Encore's executive team protected their desired and dreaded images, the more their problems accumulated and the more certain Brandon became that they weren't going to cut it.

Another consequence of clinging to our desired images is that others don't suspect that we have them, which leaves us to feel alone with our vulnerabilities. Almost no one on Encore's management team realized that their teammates felt as isolated as they did. They also didn't suspect that Brandon was equally afraid of being judged. Brandon didn't even realize it yet. Everyone simply covered up when they felt hurt, or bit back with a sarcastic rejoinder.

This cycle continues until someone shares how they feel. On the final day of the seminar, I had just come over to check in when Brandon made his sarcastic comment to Sharon. Despite her tough exterior, she admitted she'd been hurt, and that moment of courage created several breakthroughs.

First, it brought vulnerable emotion into the meeting, which allowed others on the team to express similar feelings. In this case, it happened to be a woman who opened up first, but several men on the team felt even more insecure with Brandon. Second, it confronted Brandon with the real costs of his behavior. He didn't know why he did it, but he realized he didn't like its effect.

The team decision to "stop the slow poison of sarcasm" was a great first step, but the underlying issues remained unaddressed. In the coming months, with the safety valve of making fun of each other gone, perceptions and judgments at Encore piled up. Relationships on the team actually became more uncomfortable.

In this situation, who among them would be willing to let go of their desired and dreaded images and put their performance and behavioral issues on the table? Almost nobody, including Brandon. *The level of transparency of the most senior leader in any organization directly influences how safe it is for others to open up.* Brandon was dictating but not demonstrating. And since he was the boss, his lack of honesty and transparency made it extra difficult for his team to progress.

Recognizing When We Are Triggered

BRANDON

When we got back to San Diego, we kept our commitment regarding sarcasm. Sadly, it was like putting a Band-Aid on a hemorrhage. While we didn't tell people their ideas were stupid, judgments were still made. I felt annoyed, but didn't communicate it, at least not verbally. Beneath the surface, tension continued to build.

An ongoing, divisive issue was whether or not to continue our relationship with LaL. We had contracted to attend three additional seminars in 2006: February, May, and September. The majority of Encore's executives wanted no part of the February seminar. I was tired of fighting about it, so I allowed them to delay their participation until a similar program was held in July. It still wasn't optional. I found it ironic that I was pushing for a program I so disliked.

Our arguments about participating with LaL were symptomatic of a growing division within the management team. The business was increasingly challenged and the early returns of our new initiatives weren't positive. Our stock price, which traded at over $20 per share at the beginning of 2005, had dropped below $15 and would continue falling through May to a low of around $9. The newly hired leaders were defensive about the lack of progress, and the legacy executives pointed at each other when problems arose.

More and more I found myself looking to Paul and Sharon for guidance. As a threesome, we tried to identify problems and develop solutions. We spent time examining each leader and his or her team. I didn't anticipate any negative reaction from team members who were not invited to these inner-circle meetings and I didn't feel the need to be transparent about the goals of the conversations. By the middle of February, however, many of the other executives were whining to me about how they were upset that we were "talking behind their backs." Annoyed by their pettiness, I defended my process and my two confidants.

I thought all the unrest would blow over. In the spring, however, two of our most experienced executives quit, one to start a consulting practice, the other to join a fledgling company. I couldn't believe they were leaving without having a discussion with me. I had always prided myself on being somebody people wanted to work for and hadn't experienced any real turnover. Now we were forced to find new executives during a tremendously challenging time.

"Why didn't you come talk to me?" I asked one of the departing executives during his exit interview.

"I tried talking about my concerns," he said, "but you dismiss anything you don't want to hear."

I wanted to tell him that wasn't true but bit my tongue.

"You've relied on me less and less, and lately it hasn't felt like you even want me on your team," he continued. "I want to work where I'm valued, not taken for granted."

His last statement gnawed at me, and my mind fought over who was to blame. Was he a quitter—or did I fail as a leader?

I didn't have time to think this through or to deal with individual concerns, even my own. I was steering the ship in the middle of a hurricane and needed all hands on deck. We had bigger problems to overcome.

Mid-spring, given our weak stock price, our board decided we should "pursue strategic alternatives"—either take Encore private or merge with another company—in order to ensure the greatest value for Encore's shareholders. While I understood the logic, the timing was awful. Short two key executives, we were scrambling to get an international site off the ground, deal with an unprofitable core business, and fully assimilate our acquisition.

On the personal front, Dana and I were expecting our first child in July. It was an amazing gift, and I knew Dana would be a fantastic mother. It gave me something positive to focus on outside of work. I had a lot of guilt about seeing Trevor only 50 percent of the time. I marveled at his ability to go back and forth between two households without complaining. I wanted to emulate his happiness, spend more quality time with him, and treasure the arrival of my second son.

Instead, the board's strategic alternative mandate was consuming most of my and Paul's time. It seemed too much to handle. Dana's due date was forty-five days away, and my travel was increasing by the week. I felt helpless in my efforts to be present with Trevor. Dana didn't like my absences and was afraid I'd lose my job if we merged with a larger company. That hadn't even occurred to me.

SHAYNE

Our work with Encore was stalling. Four different coaches were working with the extended management team. The cliques and mistrust Encore's executives had previously identified stayed firmly entrenched and finger-pointing crisscrossed the organization. Poor performance, ulterior motives, egregious behaviors, general incompetence—much of the frustration seemed to be surfacing in coaching calls, and often two descriptions of the same event bore little resemblance. Suggestions for how the team might engage each other in direct communication went unheeded. Brandon frequently rescheduled our calls, and when we did speak, he was more interested in fixing other people's behavior than reflecting on his own.

Much of their blame for what wasn't working kept coming back at us, the ones poking the lion in the eye. I began doubting whether we should continue bringing these issues to the surface. Brandon wasn't working on his judgments or examining his contribution to the team's dynamics. It was logical that his team didn't feel enough trust to disclose their weaknesses to him. Should we really be encouraging them to do so?

As frustrated as I was with Brandon and his team, I understood how they felt. Many of the executives were caught in a kaleidoscope of unwanted circumstances. Business conditions had worsened, along with the value of their stock options; Brandon felt the pressure of delivering seemingly unreachable results; people on the team doubted Brandon's trustworthiness, and the closed-door meetings with Paul and Sharon only made it worse; several executives were grappling with difficult personal circumstances, including a divorce.

The experience Encore's leadership team was having is a familiar one to many of us, myself included. There are moments in life when we feel that *external circumstances or people are dictating our experience.* The emotions we feel in these instances are typically negative: resentful, frustrated, powerless, agitated, afraid, stressed, angry, and trapped. At LaL, we describe this experience as feeling "at the mercy" of these unwanted people or circumstances—feeling bad because *they* are doing this or *that circumstance* is to blame.

We can feel at the mercy *acutely*, like how Brandon felt when the two executives left Encore without warning, or *chronically*, like how we feel about work demands, difficult relationships, or others' or our own personality traits.

For some of us, feeling this way is so common we don't even notice it. Over the past decade, I have asked hundreds of leaders to identify what portion of their work life they spend feeling at the mercy. Most estimate being in this unwanted state of mind 95 to 98 percent of the time. A more upbeat minority sees itself as being at the mercy 70 percent, with a few outliers at 50 percent. My data aren't scientific, but these diverse groups come from all industries and walks of life.

It is neither good nor bad to be at the mercy—it is just a term to describe an experience we all have. Learning to recognize when we are in this state is very useful, however, because it is an indication that we are *reacting* to our environment, not *proactively influencing* it.

AT THE MERCY

1. My attention is on myself

2. My experience is dependent on external people or circumstances

3. I have a win–lose mindset "It's me against others"

Being at the mercy is a sign that we believe people or circumstances are threatening our success, comfort, well-being, and value. In this state we believe that if the external situation could just change, everything would be better; so, we strive to "fix" whatever seems to be causing our distress. This might seem logical, but it's frequently counterproductive. The problem is that our egosystem distorts our assessment of any threat. We read criticism, abandonment, judgment, competitiveness, and aggression into a situation where it may or may not exist. We overreact, no longer guided by the internal clarity of our authentic intentions but by fear or agitation.

Although it can seem like it, we don't always feel at the mercy. We all experience moments of calm and focus; that is, when our full attention is devoted to the task at hand and we are tapping into our full potential. Our energy and attention flow *from* us toward the world, *regardless of external circumstances or stimuli*. We call this state of mind "at the source."

However infrequently we may experience it in adulthood, at the source is actually our "natural" state—think of the simple joy of children. Unfortunately for many of us, at the mercy has become our "habitual" state. A more productive at the source mindset is *always* within you, even if external circumstances don't change. Getting there begins by recognizing when you're feeling at the mercy.

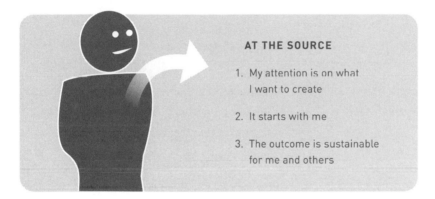

AT THE SOURCE

1. My attention is on what I want to create

2. It starts with me

3. The outcome is sustainable for me and others

Brandon and I were both feeling at the mercy of our collaboration during the spring of 2006. I felt caught between two undesirable choices: continue to encourage and cajole Brandon into working on himself—to no apparent effect—or to express my growing frustrations and risk displeasing him and losing Encore as a client. I was caught in a "damned if I do, damned if I don't" paradigm of thinking.

Brandon was in a similar lose–lose mindset. He could force his team to attend our programs, knowing he would encounter their mounting rebellion. Or he could stop the partnership, only to find himself alone with the performance and leadership issues hampering his team. Neither option seemed likely to succeed.

CHARACTERISTICS OF FEELING AT THE MERCY OR AT THE SOURCE

Below are some common characteristics of how we experience being "at the mercy" and "at the source." If you have even one of the feelings in the ATM column, it is a sign that your egosystem is triggered, and you are reacting to a perceived threat to your well-being, sense of safety, or (most frequently) your sense of value/worth.

AT THE MERCY	AT THE SOURCE
Angry	Authentic/Accepting vulnerability
Being right or wrong	Centered/Calm
Confused	Clarity
Defiant/Defensive/Doubtful (toward self or others)	Empathetic
	Energy/Enthusiasm
Fear	Engaged/Committed
Guilt	Enlarged vision
In control	Flow/In the zone
Inferior/Superior	Giving
Judging/Fearing judgment	Good for me & others
Me, me, me!	In a learning space
Numb/Not present	In reality/Accepting "what is" (as my starting point)
Obligation/"Have to"/ Should	In touch with essentials
Obsessed with getting outcome	Intention
	Joy
Pride	Letting go of outcome/expectations
Reactive	Present (for ourselves/others)
Regret/Replaying the past	Reliable/Responsible
Righteous	Supporting others
Sense of luck	Trust
Win at all costs	

This sense of being in a no-win situation is a defining character-istic of being at the mercy. It seems we have limited options, none of them good. We don't allow ourselves to explore other responses to the situation because, in some way or another, they threaten our ego's sense of worth and comfort. This trade-off is unconscious, until we address it directly.

My team and I convened a meeting to take stock of our progress with Encore, and all my fears and frustrations came out. I didn't want to irritate Brandon, so I was acquiescing to his tactics and smart rejoinders. I didn't want to appear incompetent or ineffective to my teammates, so I hadn't been talking about my struggles. One of them pushed me to acknowledge how I was taking Encore's negative aggression toward us personally.

I saw that I wasn't doing everything in my power to support Brandon and Encore to make the changes necessary for their business. Confront-ing Brandon on his behavior worried me, but it was exactly what he needed. Accepting that I could lose what was at stake for me—my image in his eyes and our business relationship with Encore—allowed me to be guided by what I wanted for Brandon and his team. They needed to address their gaps and step up to their challenges, if not with us, then with someone else.

I felt lighter and calmer when I flew down to see Brandon a few days later. Nothing had changed at the company, but I felt different on the inside. Nonetheless, when I told him we should stop working together unless he engaged differently in our partnership, I fully expected to lose Encore as a client.

BRANDON

I needed a life preserver and hoped Shayne would provide me with one when he paid me a visit in early July. Finally, somebody who would listen to my challenges and help me keep things together. Instead, he told me he and his team were fed up with our lack of adherence to our developmental goals and commitments. They had seen enough apathy and finger-pointing and wanted out of the relationship. Personally, he was tired of my convenient excuses for missing coaching appointments.

I wanted to throw him out of my office.

"Well, that was helpful," I said. "If you leave now, you can still catch an earlier flight home."

"Look," Shayne began, ignoring my sarcasm, "almost nobody on your team wants to come to our seminar next week. They feel forced by you."

"They need it! We're facing serious challenges, and they have gaps."

"You know that, and I know that. But they don't—and it can't be our job to tell them. We've become a distraction because we're pushing people to look at developmental issues they don't want to acknowledge and you're not willing to bring up."

I didn't have an answer for that.

"Which brings us to you."

We stared at each other across the conference table in my office. He wasn't angry. I didn't even read judgment on his face. If anything, he looked anxious.

"If you want change, you need to lead it. That means, first and fore-most, that you work on yourself. You must acknowledge and address your own behaviors and look for your responsibility in these dynamics. If the CEO doesn't commit, the management team will not."

"Who are you to accuse me of not being committed?" I asked him.

"Are you?"

I had been at Encore for six years. Right now, I was holding the company together. Without me, what would happen? And yet . . . my divorce, my lack of reliability, my judgments. Maybe I was just committed on my terms?

Shayne was holding up a mirror to my denial as well as my insecurities. I didn't like his message, but I sensed it was true. I intellectually knew that change came from the top, but I hadn't been willing to talk about, much less actively work on, my critical shortcomings. I was afraid that if I acknowledged my flaws, the management team would lose faith in me and the board would find somebody else to be CEO. I knew there was a case to be made for hiring a new leader. Our stock was down 50 percent, the new ventures weren't taking off, the international site wasn't getting any traction, and the pricing for assets remained at all-time highs. We were heading toward a crisis, and I needed to try something different.

"OK," I said, "I'm in. Where do we start?"

With nothing to lose, I began truly partnering with LaL to work on myself. I committed to biweekly coaching calls and a full day meeting with Shayne each quarter. At his suggestion, I also agreed to attend their seminar again in November. Like repeating a course you flunked—except it felt energizing instead of remedial. It was a pivotal moment in my career.

CHAPTER 2

NO, IT'S NOT JUST YOUR PERSONALITY

We Learned to Behave This Way

BRANDON

After my conversation with Shayne, I went home and spoke with Dana. Over a glass of wine, I told her what an impactful meeting I had earlier that day. I was excited about my commitment to make real improvement in my leadership gaps and help Encore achieve its full potential.

"Are you flipping serious?" Dana said to me. "You've had the past eight months to work on these issues and *now* you want to get serious? Can't you think of anybody but yourself?"

When I signed up for four additional weeks of travel on top of my current commitments, I hadn't considered one important variable: her due date was less than ten days away. When she finished lambasting me, I told her it would be fine. "I'll find a way to balance everything."

I slept on the couch that night.

Dana was right, of course. I was focused on myself. I was obsessed with finding a way to navigate the mounting challenges at Encore. Pricing for new portfolios continued to increase. For every dollar we collected, we spent fifty-five cents in operating expenses. To be consistently profitable, that needed to drop by 20 percent.

Complicating everything was the strategic review process initiated by the board in May. Instead of focusing on running the business, Paul and I spent significant time meeting with private equity groups and other potential suitors, including our competitors. In one memorable meeting, the chairman of another public company explained that his company had the formula for long-term success and we would benefit from being part of *their* team. Paul and I were shocked. We thought they would be one of the first to fail and we had the enduring model. But our recent results didn't back up our assessment. Were we completely wrong? Was it possible that an inferior competitor could acquire us? It would be months before these questions would be resolved. In the meantime, I needed to concentrate on delivering results for our shareholders and improving my team's leadership abilities.

My son Aidan was born in mid-July. Dana was adjusting well to being a full-time mom, and Trevor was a very engaged big brother. Encore muddled through its key initiatives, but somehow our stock price actually rebounded nicely. It allowed me to feel a little less frantic when I arrived in Sausalito in November for LaL's leadership seminar.

This time, I came with three new Encore executives. While the location was the same, my approach was different. Instead of looking for reasons to disengage, I focused on tackling my shortcomings.

We spent the first few days working through exercises designed to identify the causes of our unproductive behaviors. Sometimes, these exercises asked us to reflect on our childhood. I quickly identified important moments, but I couldn't connect them with specific feelings. It was frustrating.

One behavioral issue *was beginning to stand out*: my inability to deliver critical feedback to people in a constructive way, even if I knew they would ultimately fail without it. Because I was outspoken and thrived on debate, I had never perceived myself as avoiding conflict. Over the past year, however, as I sought to stop using sarcasm, I realized I had a lot of unexpressed criticisms. Instead of delivering the feedback to my team, I rationalized that people would get defensive or weren't capable of changing. I discussed this with Shayne.

"If you were struggling," Shayne asked, "would you want your boss to bring it up and help you identify a path forward?"

The obvious answer was yes. "I want to tell them what I think," I explained, "but I worry it will hurt their feelings."

"That's a common feeling. It may feel like it's about the other person, but underneath, the root cause of these behaviors is ultimately about you and your self-worth. How would hurting their feelings be a threat to your ego?"

I thought out loud, "Well, if they feel hurt, they might shut down or get defensive—"

"And so, how would that make you uncomfortable or threaten you?"

I paused, thinking about my CFO, Paul, with whom I now had a warm relationship and increasingly strong collaboration. There were certain leadership behaviors I didn't raise with him because I didn't like the awkward silence that fell between us. "The threat to my ego would be that they wouldn't like me."

"And what would be the danger of that?"

I felt tension in my chest as I pictured it in my mind. "Separation. Rejection."

"Can you feel that discomfort now, as you say that?"

I nodded.

"That's your key. That underlying fear of separation is what's stopping you."

I challenged myself to remember when I had felt that same discomfort growing up. It dawned on me that I'd frequently felt it during visits with my mother's parents.

I always loved being around my maternal grandparents, especially my grandfather, who took me fishing and taught me how to play golf. Time with them at their home in Florida was often the highlight of my summer. But the relationship between my parents and my mother's mom and dad was tense, and long periods passed when they didn't speak with one another. On one visit, they had a huge argument. In the middle of the night, my parents woke up my brother and me, packed the car, and drove us back to New Jersey in a rage.

My parents didn't speak with my grandparents for months. It wasn't the first time they had severed a family relationship, and usually I didn't care. But I was much tighter with my grandfather than with my other relatives, and feeling cut off from him was scary. I could see my mom wanted us on her side, and I felt caught in the middle. I finally wrote my grandparents a letter stating that if they didn't apologize I wouldn't speak to them again. Somehow, I sensed they would give in first. They did, and we went about life like it never happened.

I hadn't thought about those events in decades. I didn't know if my recollection of the facts was completely accurate, but I knew this memory was meaningful. I realized I couldn't remember a single example of a conflict leading to a useful outcome. Mapping these experiences on one of LaL's charts helped me identify conclusions I was still holding on to: "conflict leads to separation"; "you can be disposed of at any time"; "my most important relationships can just end."

Was it possible that my unwillingness to give feedback to my coworkers was tied to something that happened twenty-five years earlier? From the beginning of my relationship with Shayne, I had stayed skeptical of the notion that my past could impact my present in a dysfunctional way. *Shit*, I thought, *maybe they're right.*

SHAYNE

Brandon didn't need me to tell him to provide clearer developmental feedback. He knew it was important. So why wasn't he doing it?

Any time we know intellectually what to do, but our actual behavior is inconsistent or in contradiction, it is a sign we are being short-circuited by our egosystem. These behavioral derailers come in many forms: conflict avoidance, procrastination, defensiveness, people pleasing, shutting down, being argumentative, just to name a few. Upon examination, *these ingrained knee-jerk reactions invariably prove to be predictable and recurrent.*

Many of us can feel powerless—we see our unwanted behavior but feel unable to change it—because these behaviors seem like a fixed part of our personality. This is partially true, because these reactions are symptoms of deeper triggers. If we don't address their cause, they won't change. But when we understand why these reactions started in the first place, they become quite malleable.

Young Brandon experienced lots of conflict and arguing over the course of his childhood. He remembered some moments and forgot others. The particular fight between his parents and his grandparents stood out as significant.

When we are children, moments of disconnection, fear, and pain are scary for us, and our natural survival instinct is to prevent them. So we draw conclusions about what happened and how to avoid dangers like this in the future. Without this ability, we wouldn't survive long in the world. If we burn our hand in boiling water, our brain retains the memory of that pain, and we learn to not do it again.

The problem lies in the quality of the lesson. As children, we usually lack perspective and maturity, causing us to draw incomplete, even limiting conclusions. Worse, we are rarely explicit, even with ourselves, about the conclusions we make. In Brandon's experience, conflict and arguments were linked with rejection, separation, and out-of-control communication. Fear of reexperiencing this became one of his egosystem's "hot buttons." When he perceived that a sensitive comment might not be well received, his instinctual impulse was to move away from it. Over time, this avoidance pattern became so routinized he didn't think about it.

Part of what causes us to continue these behavioral patterns, even though we'd often prefer they go away, is that they provide us with perceived "ego" benefits. In Brandon's case, by not engaging his colleagues in uncomfortable developmental conversations, he escaped, *in the short term*, his egosystem's fear of separation, rejection, or feeling wrong about his point of view. Why bother talking about an issue if you know it'll only make things worse?

But these reactions also carry costs. By avoiding these conversations, Brandon didn't help his colleagues grow. Over time, he drew judgmental conclusions about them, fell into sarcastic humor to relieve his pent-up frustration, and decided they simply couldn't cut it at Encore. His colleagues sensed that judgment and were more quickly on guard or defensive with him. Several executives left. In the end, *Brandon's reactions produced the very outcomes he most wanted to avoid:* separation and damaged relationships.

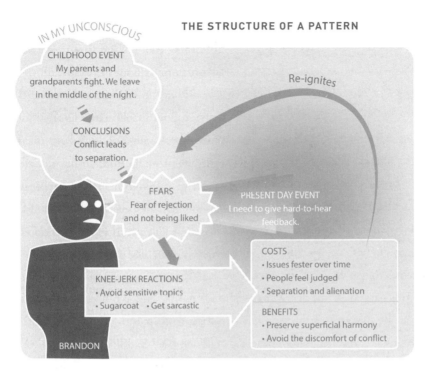

As I face certain life events, I interpret it through the lens of my FEARS. These anxieties come from CONCLUSIONS I draw from CHILDHOOD EXPERIENCES, and automatically trigger predictable KNEE-JERK REACTIONS. All this happens in my unconscious: My experience is that "I'm just responding to the situation," when in reality my action is at the mercy of my fears. When I examine the impact of this pattern in my life, I realize that the short-lived BENEFITS are look-alikes, because they mainly seek to reassure my ego. The long-term COSTS are that I create exactly what I fear or least want. Each time I play out this pattern, it reconfirms my childhood conclusions, putting me in a heightened state to reinterpret my fears in the future.

This is not a coincidence, and it is a crucial takeaway in examining your own patterns of behavior. For example, when I was younger, I was a "pathological" procrastinator. I thought my lack of discipline was a personality flaw and felt powerless to change it. Underneath this story, however, were fears: of being stupid, incompetent, and not measuring up. I would put assignments off until the last minute, then crank them out in a flurry of stressed-out productivity. I turned in decent work, always on time—but not at the level of excellence I wanted. This behavior had a highly addictive ego benefit: My laziness was to blame for my poor results, not my intelligence. But the pattern also confirmed my suspicion that I *couldn't* do excellent work. I was creating exactly what I most feared. All of this, like for Brandon, was completely hidden from me until I examined the egosystem fears behind my reactions.

Although Brandon's example is about avoidance, these egosystem mechanisms function identically for leaders who are aggressive, argumentative, or abrasive. Knee-jerk reactions that overpower others can help us maintain feelings of control or invulnerability. Upon examination, these "fight" behaviors have ego threats—such as being wrong, appearing weak, or being hurt—similar to those for avoidance behaviors.

Because our reactive behaviors stem from painful childhood experiences, trying to use willpower to change them is like instructing ourselves to put our hand back into the boiling water. No matter how much we tell ourselves to just have that conversation, or ask for help, or not overreact, it seems too dangerous. *Our ego hot buttons have made our level of tension disproportionate to reality; we experience the danger as more threatening than it is.* Being explicit about his fears helped Brandon revisit his past experiences with adult eyes and challenge his limiting conclusions. He would ultimately begin to test the "boiling" water and discover it was lukewarm at most. This is the first step in the shift.

What Matters More Than Our Ego

BRANDON

On the third evening of the seminar, we were organized into teams so we could give feedback to one another. I had tried to get peers to give each other feedback in the past, and it always went poorly. People were either too vague or somebody got defensive and the conversation created more tension.

At the outset of the process we were instructed to share our fears about how we might be judged and what our goals were for each other. Hearing each team member's concerns made us feel closer. Rather than focusing on our opinions about each other, we outlined the challenges facing Encore and identified skill gaps and counterproductive behaviors each executive needed to address to achieve our goals. It was a chance for me to put the last few days of reflection to the test.

To my surprise, the discussion rapidly became incredibly specific, but in a constructive way. One executive told another he had a hard time following his explanations and, as a result, worried about his ability to give clear direction to his team. Another member described behaviors he thought undermined his peer's ability to drive results. Instead of reacting, the team sought to understand each other's perspectives and how they could be better leaders. I challenged myself to offer all my feedback with the intent of helping them grow. We developed a powerful sense of being "in it together."

Although the discussions seemed to progress quickly, we suddenly realized it was 11:00 pm and we were the only group left in the room. I didn't know if that made us the most in-depth team or the most screwed up. We agreed to finish in the morning before breakfast.

I was the last person to receive feedback and I worried the group wouldn't be as honest with me as they were with each other. I could recall very few times when somebody had the courage to give me critical feedback. Of the current executives, only Sharon seemed willing to do so. But the openness of the session had built trust among us, and they had no reservations.

They had three areas of concern about me. First, they didn't think I made tough personnel calls. It was clear to them that we needed to significantly improve performance on the executive team if we were going to reach our objectives and achieve consistency across departments. Second, they felt that too often I believed I was right and didn't allow for open discussions. They wondered if I was willing to change my mind. And third, they felt that I hadn't fully transitioned into the role of CEO because I wasn't delegating to a broad enough group of people and empowering them to do their jobs.

Unlike the year before, I found myself embracing the feedback rather than arguing. I was grateful for their candor and felt a measure of relief knowing they still respected my leadership despite these areas for improvement. I spent the rest of the seminar exploring these topics.

As I left, I asked Shayne to help me continue the process of giving candid, respectful feedback to my team. A month later, he and I adapted the process from the seminar to create a vision for each direct report. Two of my direct reports weren't performing well enough to continue working long term at Encore. For them to have any chance of succeeding, I needed their level of urgency around closing their skill gaps and eliminating counterproductive behaviors to match mine.

Shayne and I had identified my tendency to back off or sugarcoat my feedback if the conversation got tense. I wanted to be thorough, so he had me prepare a written document to share with each person. Knowing I would give them a copy of the document at the end of the meeting took away my "exit door." I was committed to addressing everything.

My first meeting was with a direct report who was overly critical of his peers. He had never acknowledged how disruptive he was, and I was determined to break through his resistance. When he tried to disagree early in our discussion, I told him to stop talking and just listen.

"You're stubborn and arrogant," I said, "and half the time you're totally wrong about the points you argue!"

Now that we were finally having the conversation, my pent-up frustration was released. When he raised his voice, I raised mine higher. When he tried to give his point of view, I told him I was tired of hearing his excuses. He left our meeting quite unhappy.

"Well, that went great," I said sarcastically to Shayne, who had been observing. "I can't wait for the next one."

"How were you feeling when you started the conversation?" Shayne asked. "You looked tense."

I nodded. "He's always defensive like that. Usually I tell myself life is too short, and let it go. This time, I was geared up to take him on."

"I wonder if it didn't contribute to his reaction. You had an edge in your tone, and your language was fairly harsh. In his shoes, I would have felt judged."

"Maybe, but I just don't think he is going to put in the effort, and he isn't self-aware at all."

"We have two key lessons here. First, there's an important difference between your observations and your judgments. Judgments are fixed in nature: Someone is 'that' way—incompetent, stupid, arrogant. 'They don't get it.' Our judgments are vague and threatening and usually cause others to shut down or get defensive.

"Observations, on the other hand, are what you see. Think about what a camera might record." He reached for my feedback notes on the table between us. "Let's take Dave. 'Struggles to understand the financial drivers of the business, which leads to poor operational decisions.' We've captured your evaluation in more neutral terms. But that's not usually what you say about him, is it?"

"No," I admitted. "I tend to think, 'He doesn't get numbers,' or 'He isn't analytical.'" I smiled ruefully. "That's on a good day."

"OK, so I want you to practice expressing the issues you observe instead of your summary judgments of the other person's capacity."

I nodded. "And the second point?"

"Let's come back to your edge," Shayne said. "We've been focusing on the anxieties that cause you to avoid these difficult conversations. Did those anxieties go away when you were 'gearing up' for that last discussion?"

"No. If anything, they were more intense."

"That's a crucial insight. As long as your anxieties are at play, they'll undermine your behavior. Either you'll avoid the conversation, or if you do have it, you'll be harsh or overbearing."

"So what's the solution?"

"Well, why do you want to have this conversation? What's your goal?"

"It's my responsibility. I need to have it."

"That's why you're supposed to do it," he pushed back. "But what is your intention for the other person? Why do you care?"

I hesitated. I was mostly preoccupied with my concerns about having the conversation, and my frustration at not doing it. I realized I had lost contact with why it mattered in the first place.

"They trusted me in coming to work at Encore. They need my honesty to grow."

I remembered my experience giving feedback in the seminar. The exercises and coaching pushed the team and me to put our fears aside and really focus on helping each other. The quality of our dialogue had been totally different. That was the mindset I wanted to re-create.

My second meeting was with Dave, and I was committed to expressing my observations and helping him learn and grow.

"The company is at a pivotal juncture right now," I said simply, "and I'm worried that you won't be successful without making significant improvement. My goal for our conversation today is to collectively create a plan that addresses these issues."

I spent a few minutes going through my observations. I was simultaneously more direct and less irreverent, but Dave wasn't hearing any of it. "Why wasn't I told this before?" he protested. "Some of the developmental challenges you listed are strengths of mine. They got me here, and you've told me in the past that you appreciated these strengths. Plus, the two examples you gave were totally out of context."

My first reaction was to tell him he was an idiot and end the conversation. I took a deep breath and recognized the tension rising in my chest.

Before responding, I thought about how our difficult conversations in Sausalito had brought us closer together. *I don't want him to fail,* I thought, *because I haven't been straight with him. And I don't want to break off the connection.* I refocused on being "in it together" with him.

Thinking about his comments, I realized he was right. I hadn't said these things and had previously given him positive feedback about areas similar to what I was now criticizing.

"I agree that some of this might come as a surprise," I said. "I avoided having this discussion because I was afraid it might go poorly. These conversations are hard for me, and I apologize. Despite that, I want to help you and I really need you to hear me on these issues."

Dave paused and then asked me to go back and clarify a few points. We began talking instead of arguing. By the end, we understood each other better and started defining a path forward.

SHAYNE

Brandon's feedback discussions with his executives illustrate the trap most of us fall into when trying to make personal change. We focus on the "right" behavior, which we typically think of as the opposite of our usual reaction. If we avoid conflict, we think we "just need to say what we think." If we get angry, we "just need to control ourselves." If we procrastinate, we "just need to do it." Brandon's fears of rejection and separation had caused him to delay these conversations. When he finally *willed* himself to have them, however, these and other anxieties made him more tense and "amped up." He got some things off his chest, but his accumulated frustration and judgments made him harsh. Unless we address the underlying anxiety, pushing ourselves to do the opposite or "right" behavior is usually just hindering progress in another way. The leverage to move beyond our dysfunctions lies rather in *stepping out of the reactive state of mind that triggers them.* This shift comes in stages.

First, Brandon had to acknowledge his dysfunction without hedging: He avoided difficult discussions. Then he recognized the emotional blocks that prevented him from behaving as he wanted to. Tying these fears back to his childhood allowed him to understand why they were so potent for him.

Next, instead of telling himself he "should" do the opposite, Brandon clarified his goal. He connected with the deeper intentions motivating him to have these uncomfortable conversations. What was at stake? Why did he care? What were his intentions for Dave? His goals gave him *emotional* clarity—a profound sense that he *wanted* to take the risk to share his perspective to support Dave and see him grow.

This is the essence of shifting from at the mercy to at the source, and sustainable, natural behavior change occurs in this moment. For Brandon, his decision to be "in it together" with his team was his first inspiring step to prioritize creating authentic, stable relationships over protecting his ego.

We need to proactively search for this emotional clarity; only rarely does it surface on its own. If I were to ask whether your true goals or your egosystem-driven fears were most important, you would of course say the former. Intellectually it's easy to decide that learning, growing, or creating authentic relationships is more important than not appearing incompetent, failing, or being hurt. *Unfortunately, this is not how we feel at a visceral level, or we wouldn't be continually repeating these dysfunctional behaviors.* Transformation comes when we consciously connect with goals *not tied to our self-worth* and use this emotional clarity to inspire action in the present moment.

We can tell what types of goals are guiding us by paying attention to how we feel. When we feel at the mercy, it's a sign that the self-worth concerns of our egosystem are engaged. When we are grounded in our deeper intentions or desires, we feel at the source: calmer, more inspired, more connected to a sense of meaning or purpose. For many of us, the stress of feeling at the mercy is so quasi-permanent that we've forgotten what inspiration feels like.

Our strengths and skills can be either a lethal weapon for our egosystem or a productive tool for our goals. Among Brandon's greatest strengths were his intelligence and ability to articulate his thoughts. Hijacked by his egosystem, these natural talents helped him win debates, triumph over people, and convincingly explain why he shouldn't bother having certain developmental conversations. When used in the service of his goal to mentor his team and create deeper relationships, however, these same talents allowed him to identify and express keen observations for his executive team. His assessments became insightful instead of judgmental. When Dave reacted negatively, Brandon's talents helped him move the conversation forward instead of shutting Dave down.

GOALS THAT HELP US TO BE "AT THE SOURCE"
....

When our goals stem from what really matters to us, we naturally feel the inspiration of being "at the source." On the contrary, self-worth goals invariably trigger "at the mercy" feelings. Here are a few examples of non-self-worth goals. Feel free to use these questions when getting ready for any situation.

- **Learning goals:** How is this situation an opportunity for me to grow, to expand my perspective, or to develop new skills?

- **Connection goals:** What do I want to create in my relationship with this other person or with my team?

- **Contribution goals:** What is my intention for the other person or for the larger set of stakeholders? What matters to me beyond my own success?

- **Being goals:** How do I want to show up in this situation? What behaviors or state of being will most help me step out of my own dysfunctions and support others to move beyond theirs?

It goes without saying that no leader, *including your boss*, purposefully wishes to judge a colleague instead of supporting him or her. But our behavior is always consistent with our most strongly held goal; by default, particularly in moments of stress, our egosystem makes that about self-preservation. When we can connect to other, more essential goals, we change our focus and state of being and gain access to the powerful energy of feeling at the source. As the concerns of our egosystem fall by the wayside, we draw more fully on our strengths and talents, and more productive behaviors follow. We lead with inspiration and awaken the inspiration in those around us.

Correcting Our Behaviors Before They Happen

BRANDON

The performance discussions led to real improvement among most of my direct reports. Even though I was buoyed by their progress, Encore's business prospects at the beginning of 2007 were still bleak. I couldn't believe our competitors were generating positive financial returns at the current levels of portfolio pricing, and I had expected things to ease up by now. Most of them spoke glowingly of their financial performance, and it seemed like a new corporation joined the industry every week. We watched as they kept bidding prices ever higher. At some point it had to break, but when? Our stock continued taking a beating, down from $12 in January to $9 by the end of March. Paul and I talked openly with our analysts and shareholders and asked for patience. Instead, their frustration increased. Encore was apparently the only company in the industry with a gloomy outlook.

While we couldn't control market pricing for portfolios, we could afford to pay more if we lowered our operating costs. Unfortunately, our one transformative cost savings opportunity, the call center in India, was going nowhere fast. Eighteen months after the site opened, individual performance was low and attrition was sky high. It took three hires to produce one productive employee, an unsustainable 200 percent turnover rate. Most of my U.S. leadership team wanted to throw in the towel on the experiment. I didn't, if only because we had no other options.

I was hoping for any sign of improvement when we held our quarterly India business review in late April. The meeting followed a

47

predictable script, and we quickly found ourselves in the hundredth discussion about why we missed our collection forecast. The Indian team whined about the lack of collectable accounts, and the U.S. team talked openly about the limited international skill set. I stopped listening to the repetition until a senior leader at the India site, Manu Rikhye, forcefully voiced his objections. "These telecom accounts you've given us are very low quality—what do you expect us to collect?"

"Look, Manu," I jumped in, "I don't need you to collect on our quality accounts. We can do that profitably in the U.S. I need you and your team to collect on accounts that we can't afford to work here. That's the whole point of our operation in India: cost savings."

"How can you win a boxing match with one hand tied behind your back?" he insisted.

I love talking in metaphors, but this one annoyed me. If Manu was making excuses, how would he ever hold his team accountable?

"I can't give you better accounts until your turnover is under control and your collections improve."

"We've tried that formula for eighteen months. Our turnover is high because the accounts are so terrible, people can't be successful. If you want this to succeed, give us more valuable accounts. I promise we'll deliver."

I shook my head at him through the videoconference. There was no way his team could meet our collection expectations. Giving them quality accounts would be throwing money down the drain. Still . . . what choice did I have?

I finally agreed to assign them some accounts identical to those being serviced in the United States. Enough to appease Manu, but not so many that it would hurt us when they weren't successful.

The one bright spot in the spring of 2007 was the board's decision to stop exploring strategic alternatives. After almost a year, they determined nobody was willing to pay a sufficient premium on our current stock price to make it compelling to merge or go private. We would stick to our strategic plan. Paul and I were glad to put the distraction behind us.

What I didn't know was that Nelson Peltz was negotiating with a new investor group to sell his remaining investment in the company. In early June, our two largest shareholders sold approximately 40 percent of the company to this new group. As a result, three board members resigned.

Within a month, we elected four new board members who had no track record with me; instead, they would be watching carefully to ensure I generated a return on their hundred-million-dollar investment. It seemed to happen at the worst possible time. Our strategic initiatives were still struggling, the management team was in flux, and pricing for portfolios kept rising.

At our first board meeting after the change, one of the new members looked at me and declared, "All companies need to be great at something. As far as I can tell, we aren't."

I glanced at Paul, not sure what to think.

"You need to quickly figure out what that is and get focused," he continued. "Without that, we'll need to make some changes."

It wasn't a threat, but a reality check. These new investors were not going to be satisfied with the status quo. I worried what they'd think when they heard I was attending a leadership seminar in the next thirty days. I thought about postponing, but now, more than ever, I needed to accelerate my development.

The seminar started slowly for me. I found myself preoccupied and unable to concentrate. Aidan was a year old, the new board wanted results, and Dana and I had just found out that we were expecting a daughter in February 2008. It seemed the only constant was significant change.

On the fourth day, a seemingly trivial moment caused my experience to take a major detour. We were working through an exercise when

Noah Nuer, the CEO of LaL, told the group we had thirty minutes until lunch. It was a beautiful day and I was looking forward to taking a walk along the bay to get some fresh air and gather my thoughts. Five minutes before the break, Noah told us if we weren't finished with the exercise, we could complete it during lunch. They were moving on to a new topic in the afternoon.

I was pissed. He hadn't mentioned this in his previous announcement, and now I had to change my plans. I skipped the walk and finished the exercise, but I fumed for the rest of the day. Was Noah terrible at managing time, or had he purposefully misled us? Either way, I wasn't going to stand for it.

I was still annoyed later that night in my hotel when I realized I'd had a "pinch," LaL's term for an emotional reaction. A presentation the previous day had outlined the distinction between reality, perceptions, and thoughts. One of the key conclusions was "Facts don't make us mad; it's our thoughts about those facts that do." It seemed overly simplistic, and I thought they made too big a deal of it. But twenty-four hours later, I jumped straight into the trap.

So Noah changed the schedule—why did I have so much emotion about it? With everything I was dealing with at work, who cared about such a tiny detail? After some journaling, it dawned on me that behind my resentment at missing my walk was a judgment I'd had of myself: Everybody else was getting their work done, but I was lagging behind. The other participants would surely see me sitting alone at the table while they were able to go to lunch; I was the dunce CEO of the seminar.

Over the next few days, I developed important connections between my past and my reaction to Noah. I realized that during my childhood, I'd felt a constant competition to be number one. I was the oldest kid in my family, and my grandfather always told me I was his favorite grandson. While I received positive reinforcement, my brother, Keith, was ridiculed. He never seemed to measure up and faced harsh judgments for many of his life decisions. I had added to that pile of criticisms, always deeming him lazy and unmotivated. Only now did I see how much better I felt when he was judged to be less than me. I felt sad and ashamed about how he was treated and wished I had acted differently.

This need to be the best helped explain my antipathy toward Noah. He was the only other person in the seminar with the same title as me. Since only one of us could be the "best" CEO, we were in a competition—except he didn't know it. My mind was constantly searching for his flaws and trying to discredit him. *Just like with my own team,* I realized, *I need everybody to know I'm the true leader in the room.*

This theme had played out time after time in my life. The most troubling example was my departure from my prior employer, Capital One. For the first decade after college, I was a rising star, leading thousands of employees and reporting directly to the president. When the company recruited at college campuses, my story was the example they touted as what was possible. I was influencing critical decisions and had tremendous access to the CEO. The sky was the limit—until I threw it all away in 1997.

Given its tremendous growth, Capital One decided to bring in a series of more experienced leaders, and I vehemently argued that these new hires were destroying the culture. As more outsiders took senior leadership positions, the conflict escalated until I finally resigned. These people couldn't possibly know what we stood for.

Upon reflection at the seminar, I realized it wasn't about that at all. I hadn't been able to admit that I was afraid these new leaders would outperform me. Once the president and the CEO realized I couldn't measure up, they would reject or demote me. I couldn't let that happen, so I quit! It seemed ridiculous now, but I had been blinded by the need to protect my status as the chosen one.

That was an extreme example, but the pattern was at play even today at Encore. I hired talented people, but nobody good enough to replace me. My constant judging of others ensured that I always came out on top, at least in my mind. I was dumbstruck by how many times I unwittingly fought to be number one or left the situation when I couldn't be. So many wasted learning opportunities.

SHAYNE

Our reactions are completely within our power to influence and change. Learning to notice when our egosystem is triggered, accepting these feelings with empathy, and then reconnecting to our deepest goals and intentions brings us back to a more centered state of being. We move from being at the mercy to being at the source, from being reactive to proactive and creative. *With practice, we can become aware enough of our underlying ego threats to consistently preempt our reactions before they happen.* Let me present a concrete tool that will allow you, just as Brandon did, to make this shift.

The first priority is to be attuned to when and how we feel at the mercy, and it turns out these feelings start at precise moments. Brandon was diligently working on an exercise in the seminar, and his attention was focused on how he wanted to grow as a leader. And then, in an instant, he was angry with Noah. There was a before and an after. We call the experience of this transition a "pinch." Like a physical pinch on our arm, an emotional pinch is our body reacting physiologically to an unwanted threat or circumstance.

When we experience a pinch, we have familiar sensations or symptomatic reactions that we can learn to recognize. For some people, their ears get hot, or they blush, or their stomachs knot. Brandon felt anger and resentment, and he became judgmental and critical. I typically feel a jolt of adrenalin in my chest and find myself talking faster and louder.

For others, however, noticing a pinch can be more difficult. People who are even-keeled don't always have obvious physiological or behavioral symptoms. It doesn't mean they don't have pinches, but more than likely their egosystems respond by minimizing or numbing the threat.

When we have a pinch, we think the triggering event is the cause of our reaction: what someone said or did, what we said or did, caused an unwanted outcome. For Brandon, the triggering event was Noah's announcement. But his pinch actually happened because he had *injected judgments about his self-worth* into the situation. Identifying how we each do this is critical because our mind chatter when we are pinched is often a red herring. We churn out judgments, stories, and semi-sophisticated justifications that displace our real discomfort of feeling inferior. The key to defusing our reactive behaviors is learning to identify the more primal and childish interpretation underneath.

Identifying and challenging these ego threats matters because *we are at our least effective, and most destructive, when our egosystem is triggered.* For the rest of that afternoon, "being right" over Noah had usurped Brandon's goal of developing himself as a leader. This mundane seminar example illustrates how we derail ourselves. In our daily life, we can cause far more extensive damage. As Brandon described, he actually left a lucrative job at Capital One because of the perceived threat to his ego.

Even though our reactions can seem sudden and too intrinsic to change, they are predictable. When we "sort" a pinch, we can dissect each piece of what happened as well as identify how to return to an at the source mindset.

Brandon had a pinch with his CFO Paul in the early days of working together that illustrates this process. During a critical meeting with a potential strategic buyer, Brandon noticed that the PowerPoint deck they were using was different from the one he had prepped the day before. Thrown off, Brandon stumbled through the presentation, angrily surmising that Paul had changed it to make himself look good.

When Brandon and I later broke down what happened, we identified his ego threats. This was right in the midst of his son being born; Brandon had been working fewer hours and was feeling self-conscious about not pulling his weight. After he left work the night before the meeting, Paul and his team had further revised the presentation. When Brandon discovered the unfamiliar document, it affected his ability to come off as the smartest person in the room. These familiar triggers made him defensive and accusatory.

I asked him to "reframe" his perspective by extracting his ego threats from the situation. If no one was judging him—deciding whether or not he was number one was irrelevant—how would he characterize what happened?

This step of reframing our perspective without our value involved can be difficult because we are often so blinded by this tension that we can't see much else. Brandon was able to identify that an equally valid perspective was that his team was driving things forward on their own. They were proactive and accountable, and he wasn't alone with everything that needed to get done. Instead of feeling annoyed, frustrated, and embarrassed, Brandon felt grateful. We know we have shifted our perspective when we actually feel a change in our emotional state, from at the mercy to at the source. Moreover, this event reminded him that one of his developmental goals was to "leverage the experience of his team." Sorting his pinch revealed to him that his ego's need to be number one was directly limiting his ability to unlock the full potential of his team.

In this sense, *the goal is not to avoid having pinches, but rather to notice and welcome them as opportunities to be more fully on our path of growth.* The chart that follows shows the steps in sorting a pinch and using an awareness of our triggers to more fully embrace our highest self.

REACTIVE PATH VS. SORTING A PINCH

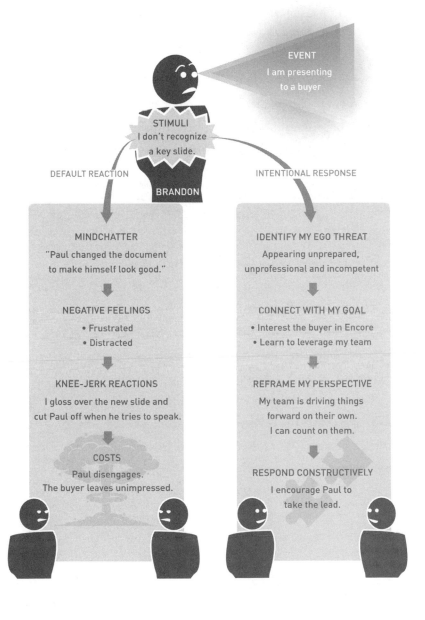

BRANDON

I had many insights during the seminar, as if I had tapped into a part of my brain that had been closed off for a long time. It crystallized on the second to last day as I wrote a note to Shayne. I saw in a personal and palpable sense how my need to be liked and admired was so strong that I made other people feel the pain I most wanted to avoid. I rejected before being rejected; I judged others when I felt judged. I often went to the point of blaming others for failures I couldn't acknowledge. It was a moment of great sadness for me. I couldn't remember the last time I cried in front of anybody except Dana. Here, however, there was no embarrassment, just clarity.

On the flight back to San Diego, I decided that it was important to talk with my team about what I learned. I prepared an outline and practiced it. I would give them a glimpse into my fears, how they were impacting the team, and enlist their support.

But when I gathered my direct reports and several other pivotal leaders in the conference room by my office, all of my planning went out the window. I didn't know what they were expecting to hear from me, but as I looked at them, fresh tears built up in my eyes. I abandoned my prepared speech and simply shared in unvarnished form what I'd seen. I apologized for how I had behaved in the past and committed to make the changes necessary to lead Encore forward. I hadn't cried in public for decades. Now it had happened twice in one week. Honestly, it was liberating.

CHAPTER 3

WORKPLACE POLITICS ARE YOUR FAULT TOO

My Reactions Create *Our* Dysfunction

BRANDON

The board's challenge to create greatness somewhere in the business was the main topic of our August 2007 strategic planning session. We felt competent, even skilled, in many areas, but not great in any. After a lot of discussion, we concluded two things should define Encore in the coming years: leveraging India and becoming the authority on our customer.

Despite the lack of traction in India, we had the opportunity to employ tremendously talented people at significantly lower wages.

Success in India would save us tens of millions of dollars annually in operating costs and be the foundation for future growth. Nothing else could have as profound an impact on the company.

We also felt that nobody really understood the people who fell deeply into debt. Characterized by words like "subprime" or "debtor," their financial troubles were attributed to an illness, loss of a job, or a divorce. But there were plenty of people who experienced these hardships and kept paying their bills. We aimed to fill that void of understanding in order to improve how we did business, how we served our customers, and the return on our investments.

We believed this combination of achievements would give Encore a sustainable cost advantage and the ability to outperform our competitors. Intellectually these priorities made complete sense to the team, but emotionally we were still reeling from our recent lackluster performance, the effects of years of significant pricing headwinds, and a lack of traction on key initiatives. Optimism had faded, and I noticed a distinct lack of energy—a resignation bordering on apathy—around the office. While my renewed commitment to work on my own dysfunctions opened my eyes to how frequently such behaviors occurred in the organization, when I pressed the leadership team to develop solutions, they seemed more focused on finding excuses for their own inaction or pointing out flaws in other people's proposals. Most new initiatives were met with resistance lower in the organization. Sharon and her Human Resources team were a favorite target, often accused of having an agenda and operating in a silo. Any initiative around benefits, training, recruiting, or employee evaluation was met with skepticism. I spent hours coaching Sharon on how to push forward without getting pushback. But it seemed like her willingness to try was matched by a collective desire to argue with her ideas.

I saw similar dynamics between our Operations, Finance, and Technology departments. The historical lack of cohesion at the executive level had created entrenched factions lower in the organization. Although our executive team was functioning better, their respective teams were still openly competing with one another and there were significant pockets of resistance to our venture in India.

Over my career, I had shrugged off this type of infighting as a normal, if unpleasant, part of doing business. But Encore's situation was becoming bleak, and I couldn't comprehend wasting time and energy on issues that didn't impact the bottom line.

Achieving our dreams for the company meant changing the mindset of many layers of management, not just the executives. I knew culture change, if even possible, would take many years to complete. I wanted to accelerate that process. Given the state of the marketplace, slow, deliberate change wouldn't be good enough.

We partnered with LaL to customize their in-house training program, called "WeLead." Leveraging insights from another round of 360-degree feedback sessions, including one for me, we identified dominant cultural dysfunctions that were holding the company back. Determined to address them, we set four key goals for the program:

1. Develop a culture of transparency around people's learning and development

2. Remove silos and "Us vs. Them" dynamics

3. Improve the level and frequency of feedback and critique of ideas

4. Transform complaining/blaming into co-responsibility

We believed that if we could achieve these outcomes, we could transform our culture and collaborate in a far more effective way.

The initial target audience was the executive team's direct reports. Over time, we planned to cascade it down through multiple layers of the organization, ultimately impacting anyone in a leadership position, or approximately 100 to 150 people.

I was hopeful that my newfound understanding of how I needed to lead differently, combined with the implementation of WeLead and our new strategic focus, would generate higher morale and profits. Only time would tell.

SHAYNE

Over the years scores of leaders have told me, "You should see the ego and politics in my organization!" Perhaps because ego-driven behaviors—people avoiding conflict or overcontrolling; personality conflicts; groups assuming ill intent or acting with a tribal mentality—are so pervasive, many leaders accept them as normal. It's the air they breathe, and they become numb to the consequences.

Learning to recognize the detrimental effects of individual egosystems on an organization's culture is the first step in addressing them. These cultural dysfunctions are complex and important enough to warrant a chapter to dissect them—what they look like, what causes them, and how they affect company performance. After this discussion, the subsequent chapters will provide tools and solutions for forging a healthier culture.

Over the past two decades, LaL has surveyed and consulted with many large organizations across dozens of industries, as well as the public, nonprofit, and academic sectors. Each organization had its own flavor, but four dominant cultural dysfunctions consistently showed up:

- Widespread *conflict avoidance*, peppered with a few leaders who are abrasive

- *Us vs. Them dynamics* (silos and turf wars, especially in matrix organizations)

- Leaders being *defensive and guarded* about developmental needs (fear of being judged)

- Employees being *reactive, tactical, and overwhelmed* by too much work

Each of these cultural derailers is triggered by self-worth fears. The employees in every one of these organizations were talented and hard-working, but they underperformed their potential in proportion to the severity of these dysfunctions. Sometimes a culture was clearly toxic, and leaders were openly hostile toward each other. In other cases, artificial harmony left key performance and operational issues unmentioned and unresolved.

Many organizations try to remove unwanted cultural tendencies through reorganizations, teambuilding outings, or redefining their mission–vision–values statements. While these efforts may produce other valuable outcomes, they rarely make significant progress on behaviors, because they don't deal with the root causes. *Cultural dysfunction is produced by many individual dysfunctions ricocheting off each other.* When leaders are defensive, territorial, artificially polite, competitive, or abrasive, it tends to trigger similarly dysfunctional behaviors in their colleagues. It doesn't matter what poster you put up on the wall. *Dominant organizational dysfunction will not decrease until individual leaders identify and overcome their personal egosystem reactions.*

Encore, for example, was a fast-paced environment where a premium was placed on analytical intelligence. Being smart, knowing the answer, and being able to defend your position effectively moved you up in the organization. These qualities—intelligence, resourcefulness, and clarity of expression—are important. Applied with other qualities to organizational goals, they can produce breakthrough results.

But recall our discussion of desired and dreaded images in chapter 1. Leaders at Encore with these qualities—like any one of us—also wanted *to be seen* as smart, competent, knowledgeable, and in control. Being wrong or asking for help felt like admitting incompetence. "If I can't do it on my own, my boss will wonder why I'm in this job," one director shared in a remark characteristic of how many at Encore felt. When protecting their desired and dreaded images became their brain's default goal—which, as we've seen, is most of the time—it eclipsed learning, collaborating with others, and doing whatever it took to meet their responsibilities. *Their unconsciously held ego goals were overriding their deeper, conscious aspirations.*

This has a social side effect. The less transparent a leader is, for example, the more dangerous it feels for his or her colleagues to reveal their own shortcomings. The less those folks are forthcoming, the more it stands out when any one person admits he or she is struggling. It is already painful enough for our ego to admit we need help; being the only one on a team to do it can feel shameful. This individual tendency to keep up a facade becomes a collective phenomenon.

At Encore, this created a cultural norm of wanting to appear to be on top of things. This may have been fine for an organization in a stable industry where success was easily achieved. But Encore in 2007 had leaders in stretch roles facing unfavorable industry trends. Not acknowledging developmental gaps meant not getting help where it mattered most.

While these tendencies often seem set in stone within an organization, they are actually quite reversible. At Encore, "developing a culture of transparency in learning and development" would become possible when a critical mass of Encore's key leaders, one by one, overcame the discomfort of their dreaded images. The more they modeled transparently requesting and accepting feedback, the more "normal" it would become—until they created a more functional cultural tendency.

How and Why We Stop Trusting

BRANDON

Besides greatness, the other deliverable we owed the board was a forecast for the remainder of 2007 and the upcoming year. We had spoken at length about the pricing pressure in the industry, and they were worried about the long-term profitability of the company if we didn't improve the cost structure. Our budgeting process usually took two months. They wanted an answer in a few weeks. Paul's office was right next to mine, so I stuck my head through his door to check in.

"How's the 2008 budget coming along? The board wants a quick turnaround. There's no time for multiple iterations."

He laughed. "Our chances of getting anything done on the first try are close to zero," he said. "It's always the same routine. The administrative departments add in a bunch of new hires we can't afford, and the ops guys set their goals so low they look like heroes when they over-deliver. Everybody postures to look good, and none of our inputs work when we roll it up to the corporate budget."

Paul had complained to me about this before. I needed to nip any delays in the bud.

"We don't have time to haggle over this," I told him. "You get your team ready, and I'll meet with the other VPs. I'll make it clear how their teams need to act and make sure the message gets to the operating leaders."

I turned to leave Paul's office just as Dave came around the corner. I asked him to come into my office.

"What am I in trouble for now?" he said jokingly.

"Nothing, I just want to talk about how we approach the planning process. I need you and your team to take Paul's guidance seriously. I—"

"Is that what you two were talking about?" he interrupted. "I'm tired of you and Paul making decisions behind closed doors and expecting the rest of us to fall in line. You should be asking me about *my* concerns. Instead, you take his side on everything."

"What are you talking about? My door is always open for you."

"It doesn't seem like it. I manage this stuff day-to-day, Brandon. I know what we're capable of doing. Paul is disconnected from what's happening on the floor. Why would you listen to him and not me?"

I was tired of hearing this from Dave. In addition to bitching about the budget process, he had recently begun complaining about our methodology for buying portfolios. One day we weren't paying enough for new portfolios, the next day our models weren't accurate. It seemed like he always had a complaint of the day and wouldn't listen to anyone who disagreed.

"If you recall, I was the chief operating officer for many years," I said irritably. "I'm keenly aware of what's happening on the floor. You're not the only person with perspective." I moved to put the conversation to bed. "I don't always agree with Paul, but this planning process will be driven by him, and I need you to follow it."

"Paul and his team of MBAs have fancy models producing numbers that look good on paper. But without my input, the whole plan is disconnected from operational reality." Dave sat back and crossed his arms. "Garbage in, garbage out."

I guess we aren't ending the discussion. I was surprised how frustrated I was. Just a short time ago, we had come together on his development plan and were solving problems as a team. Now he was resisting things that shouldn't be controversial. What was going on?

"Look," I said. "If we went with the numbers your team produces, we'd go broke."

We went back and forth for a few minutes. The more adamant he was, the more I dismissed his points.

"Why don't you value my opinion? I know this as well as anyone in the company. You're not listening."

"Do you hear yourself? When I see how little you respect Paul's Finance team, I worry about how your team is interacting with areas like Strategic Initiatives. Are you taking advantage of improvements they recommend?"

"Don't worry, Brandon. I'm not missing any opportunities because they don't produce anything useful. If they ever do, rest assured, I'll jump on it."

Not for the first time, our conversation was going nowhere fast. I wasn't reassured in the least.

SHAYNE

"Now that I understand the downward spiral I was in with Dave," Brandon said later, "I see it everywhere. It's an epidemic."

People's egosystems do more than just generate cultural dysfunction. Their desired and dreaded images and reactive behavior patterns set off ego-driven personality conflicts. These unconscious dynamics can lead to broken relationships and disrupt collaboration between individuals and entire departments.

Brandon's communication dynamic with Dave was symptomatic of many other downward spirals between leaders at Encore. Brandon thought the problem with Dave was that he was negative, stubborn, and extreme. Dave thought Brandon was biased and didn't listen to him or value his opinion. Naturally, each thought that if the other just changed the way he was behaving, their communication would improve.

Instead, when Brandon perceived Dave as being stubborn, he tuned him out. If Dave were a robot, he might have shrugged this off. As a human being, however, he had his own set of ego threats, and Brandon's behavior made him feel ignored—a powerful trigger. Feeling pinched, Dave ratcheted up his intensity and language, hoping Brandon would see the wisdom of his words. But that reaction simply frustrated Brandon more, and the opposite occurred; Brandon was even less inclined to listen. When Brandon cut Dave off, he was hoping Dave would realize his ideas were off base and change them. Instead, Dave doubled down on his position.

These loops are called "self-fulfilling prophecies," and they describe how we unknowingly invite other people to react in ways that confirm our assumptions about them, and then use those reactions to justify our initial assumptions and behaviors.

The more Brandon believed Dave was negative and stubborn, the more he noticed when Dave raised his voice or used extreme language. He missed Dave's attempts to advocate objectively. "It got to the point," Brandon laughed ruefully, "where I had dismissed his input before he even opened his mouth."

Science has extensively researched our brain's tendency to notice— or interpret—what we expect to see. It is called "confirmation bias." This forms a type of "filter" through which any information that contradicts our preconceived expectations passes unnoticed. Unfortunately, our brain doesn't alert us when it's discarding information about another person. We believe we are balanced in our perspective, when in fact the other person has a smaller and smaller window of possibility to speak to us. To make matters worse, their view of us is deteriorating in parallel, making them less and less likely to communicate in ways we can hear. Over time, self-fulfilling prophecies can make it nearly impossible for two people to have a quality discussion. The judgments and frustrations that accumulate can strain relationships to the breaking point. This downward spiral also happens in personal relationships, and our high divorce rate is proof of it. In all these cases, we experience it as entirely the other person's fault and don't see how we've actively contributed.

BRANDON-DAVE SELF-FULFILLING PROPHECY

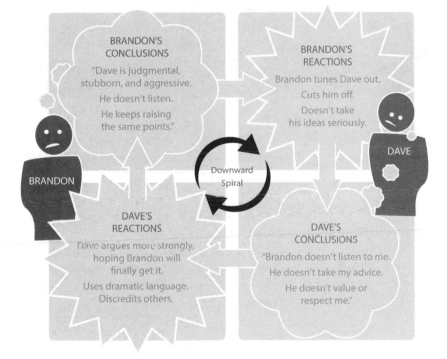

Realizing that these loops exist is a crucial first step. Unless we recognize when they occur in our daily life, we will unwittingly fall into them. The following figure outlines the generic steps of this loop.

SELF FULFILLING PROPHECY LOOP

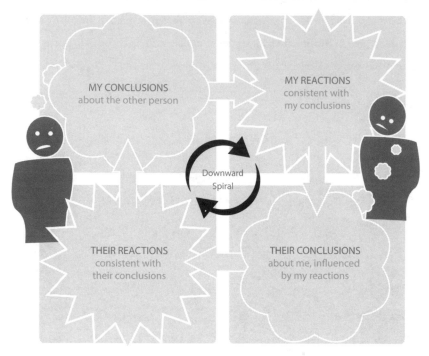

DEFAULT EXPERIENCE: I believe I am just at the mercy of the person's behavior and bear no responsibility.

SELF-AWARE EXPERIENCE: I realize that my conclusions and actions are influencing the other person to react in ways that frustrate me. If I were him/her, I would respond similarly. I can break out of this cycle by working on my beliefs and/or actions.

These downward spirals are so difficult to stop because our egosystem plays an active, pernicious role in them. It builds in stages.

First, we see something negative in another person, feel threatened or aggravated by it, and react counterproductively. In Brandon's case with Dave, he had concerns about Dave's competence and analytical ability. His fears of rejection and not being liked, however, caused him to avoid expressing his criticisms. His frustrations and beliefs built up, becoming judgments that drove his part of the self-fulfilling prophecy. So Brandon's conflict avoidance pattern contributed to the first stage of the downward spiral.

Then, the less functional their relationship became, the more it triggered other ego threats for Brandon. "I hired Dave over the concerns of Paul and a few other people," Brandon explained. "Seeing him struggle gave me a 'failure' or 'I was wrong' pinch." This discomfort came out as impatience and anger, which also fed their self-fulfilling prophecy.

Brandon was further triggered by Dave's stubbornness, setting off his fear of being wrong and his tendency to debate. There was no way he was going to concede a point to someone he judged as not smart enough to understand Encore's business.

When we add it all up, we realize that Brandon wasn't neutrally dismissing Dave because he was extreme; he was shutting him down because it made his egosystem feel right, superior, and powerful. As for each one of us, stopping his part in a self-fulfilling prophecy meant no longer reaping a variety of powerful ego benefits.

It's not that Dave didn't have performance issues and skill gaps to address. But Brandon had lost his ability to productively coach and mentor him. Despite theoretically wanting Dave to succeed, *Brandon's ego was invested in knocking him down.* Similarly, Dave knew his relationship with Brandon was crucial to his job at Encore, yet his ego caused him to be argumentative and guarded, directly undermining the likelihood of his success. All of this, to our detriment, happens unconsciously.

More problematic, this prevalent one-on-one dysfunction invariably spawns team-on-team dysfunction.

The Us vs. Them Epidemic

BRANDON

I told Paul that Dave wasn't thrilled with the process but understood the urgency. Paul called a meeting with the leadership team and their budgeting analysts. Twenty key people were needed to create the forecast.

"Welcome," Paul said. "I asked the Finance team to give us a head start by creating a collection and revenue forecast for the next eighteen months—"

Before he could get a second sentence out, one of Dave's key lieutenants cut him off.

"I don't know where these numbers come from, so how can I be sure they are accurate?"

"They come directly from our models," Paul responded. "Just like they always do."

"Yes," another operational leader spoke up, "but are they correct?"

I stopped the discussion. "Nobody can predict what will happen over the next year with 100 percent precision, but these are our best projections. We need to work with them."

I shot a look at Dave. He asked his team to hold their thoughts until Paul completed his explanation. With everybody back on task, Paul resumed the discussion.

"I am also distributing a current headcount census that is the foundation for the expense projections—"

"I haven't seen this before," another person objected. "I can't agree to use it without verifying it myself."

"Are you questioning my work?" one of Paul's financial directors asked.

Several people started talking at once. What was going on? Barely ten minutes had passed, and we were all over the place, arguing about things that weren't controversial.

"Look, guys, these numbers are accurate," I cut them off. "We need to move on."

That didn't work either.

"Every year, the Finance guys and the Decision Science people create scenarios without our input," someone from the Operations team called out in frustration. "Then you ask us to build an operating plan around numbers we don't believe in and have no ability to influence."

"Actually, you typically ignore our numbers and build forecasts that fall short of our corporate objectives," Paul said. "It helps you look good when you exceed expectations. Are we here to win a beauty contest or increase the stock price?" In this case, I thought his sarcasm was justified.

"We give you reasonable projections of what people can actually do," Dave retorted, "not made-up numbers to fit your fantasy."

The whole room was tense. Until now, I hadn't noticed the seating arrangements and nonverbal cues between groups. The Finance and Decision Science people sat on one side of the table, while the Operations and other staff leaders sat on the other. When one member of either "group" made an assertion about the other, head nodding and affirmative glances followed. Finding it unacceptable, I stepped in more forcefully.

"You *will* do a forecast using these numbers as a baseline. To Paul's point, I'm worried about past patterns of sandbagging collection objectives. We have no room for error. You guys need to make your individual targets match the portfolio expectations, period."

The meeting continued without any additional debate. People listened to Paul and then dutifully left the room.

I went back to my office, feeling troubled. Why were we having such a difficult time rallying around a basic plan? How would we ever overcome the major challenges ahead if we couldn't do the simple things quickly and efficiently? Our new investors were counting on me. I was just glad they weren't in our meetings.

SHAYNE

Paul and Dave had progressed far enough down the self-fulfilling prophecy loop that neither had much respect for the other. They dismissed the other's point of view; they defended their positions in disagreements; they were critical of each other out of earshot. The responsibilities and objectives that Paul and Dave shared, like building a useful budget or implementing operational improvements, took a backseat. This kind of dysfunction between key executives is common in large organizations.

Often having pinches with the other, Dave and Paul each talked with Brandon, other executives, and their own team about their frustrations, drawing them into the dynamic like a black hole swallowing sunshine. It's an unfortunate trait of the egosystem that we seek out people to confirm we are right rather than to challenge our perceptions. This inclusion of other people amplifies these downward spirals to an organizational level. Because both Paul and Dave led departments, their respective teams progressively saw the conflict through their leader's eyes. They developed antagonistic views not only of the other leader but also of the sister organization. By the time Brandon unwittingly sat down with these teams to create the budget forecast, this "Us vs. Them" divide had been going on for some time. The following figure schematically shows how this amplification occurs.

The conflict Brandon described between Finance and Operations was just one of many interdepartmental Us vs. Them dynamics. Sharon and her Human Resources team were exasperated with how Operations took exception to every initiative they launched; Strategic Initiatives bristled at how infrequently Operations followed through on their ideas, while Operations belittled SI's plans as naive and disconnected from reality; the middle of the organization judged senior management for their double-talk and lack of clear direction; and, of course, everyone complained about Information Technology.

I wish Encore had been an anomaly, but it wasn't. Over the last twenty years, my colleagues and I have worked with multinational Fortune 500 corporations, government agencies, privately owned companies, nonprofits, and academic institutions. Almost without exception, individuals, teams, and departments in these varied organizations developed beliefs and stories about each other, until they eventually spent significant amounts of their time and energy criticizing each other's behaviors and intentions. They saw the problem as "over there." They were right, and the other group just didn't get it. But that "other" group believed just as fervently that they were the heroes, and the first group the villains. Science calls this "self-serving biases."

People don't do this because they are stupid, or because they have bad intentions, or even because they don't know better (they usually do). Also, being aware that self-serving biases exist is insufficient to stop us, because we unconsciously depend on them. How could we not? These entrenched conflicts feed our addiction of feeling right and being the hero. They enable us to shift the blame for our shortfalls. Most delicious of all, obsessing about "them" distracts us from our most daunting business challenges. It was far more gratifying for Operations to focus on how Sharon and HR had an agenda and SI's ideas were useless than to confront their own difficulty in responding to massive price increases. And let's not forget how colluding against an outside enemy is an easy way for a group to create an artificial sense of cohesion.

This group collusion makes it doubly hard to change. As leaders, once our judgments of others are known, softening or changing our position can feel like publicly losing face, appearing weak, or being seen as a traitor to our "side." All these ego motivators contribute to how invested we become in other people or groups being wrong. This is the great tragedy of workplace politics, turf wars, and lack of trust: *nobody wants it, but everybody perpetuates it.*

HOW INDIVIDUAL SELF-FULFILLING PROPHECIES
BECOME DEPARTMENT-WIDE US VS. THEMS

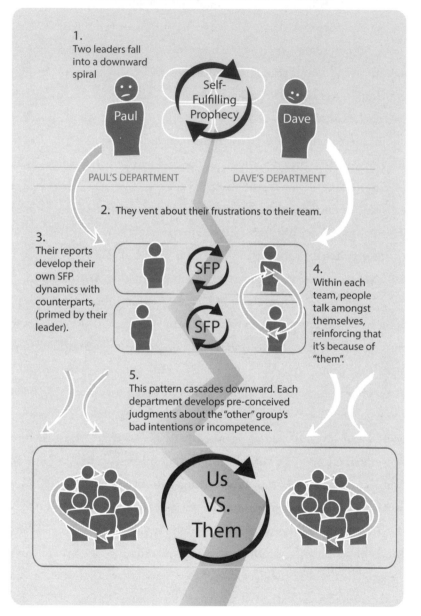

In a "functional" company, departments operate in their own silos, working around each other but not creatively collaborating. In most organizations (especially matrixed), these turf wars become disruptive, as mutual suspicion prevents problem solving or working effectively toward shared goals. When performance shortfalls occur, learning and accountability get overrun by finger-pointing. The organization's mission takes a back seat.

Unfortunately, the popular strategy of reorganizing a company or a department is ineffective at resolving silos and turf wars. The causes are not structural, so structural solutions will not fix them. More than once I have seen leaders of two warring factions exchange roles—and within three months be aggressively accusing the very people they previously led.

With these dynamics at play, functional collaboration—much less high-performance teaming—becomes nearly impossible. To make any significant and sustainable progress on these spirals, each leader needs to understand, on a personal level, how he or she has become invested in them.

What are the uncomfortable ego threats that push you to judge, criticize, avoid conflict, and/or vent to others? How does this lead you to be the starting point of these divisions in your teams and departments? What is the cost of these broken relationships to your key strategies and bottom line results? These were questions that Brandon and his team were just beginning to contemplate.

The Dollar Cost of Cultural Breakdowns

BRANDON

With the planning process finally under way, I turned my attention back to India. Our failure to get any traction was sobering, and I was desperate to change the trajectory of this very complicated venture. We were trying to motivate recent college graduates in India to collect debt from people halfway around the world. Their job consisted of making phone calls between the hours of 5:00 pm and 5:00 am to ask for sums of money most of them didn't earn in a year. Just as daunting, these employees needed approval from their families to take the job. Culturally, what someone's parents think really matters in India. Disapproval of the company or the industry meant they just didn't work there. Period.

Had it been me, I think I would have found a new profession. But Manu Rikhye and his team were determined to make it work. They were constantly brainstorming solutions and looking for the silver lining. I was so impressed with their attitude and commitment, quitting just didn't seem like an option.

I set up a meeting with Jay Cherry, our VP of Operations, to get an update on performance. Jay and I had worked together for a long time and I knew he would give me his unvarnished opinion.

"Well," Jay said right off the bat, "your test worked."

"What test?"

"When you authorized giving higher-quality accounts to our Indian collectors, we set up a small, dedicated group so we could track their progress."

"What, did we get a 5 percent or 10 percent increase?" I asked.

"You're way off. The team in India is absolutely killing it, Brandon. After only four months, they're producing revenues comparable to domestic teams."

"That can't be right. Our learning curve in the U.S. is six to seven months, and most people fail. How could India get an entire team to *average* numbers this high? You're missing something."

"I thought the same thing, so I went through the numbers myself. Math doesn't lie. They're doing something amazing. Manu was right."

I still didn't believe him. Assuming there was a clerical error or too many accounts had been sent to India, I forced Jay to take me through the numbers. Everything added up.

"Even more impressive," Jay added, "is how they're doing all this with abysmal technological support. Imagine having to make small talk for five to ten seconds because our system is painfully slow and hasn't told you whom you're talking with."

I realized with a shock that I had been a victim of my preconceived ideas. I had viewed our Indian workforce as low-cost employees capable of collecting only on marginally profitable accounts. They were a cost-reduction play and my decisions had unwittingly helped them prove me right. The mere act of doing something different had allowed them to break out of the cycle. I now realized that if I viewed them as a high-quality workforce—each Indian employee as valuable as an American employee—it became a contribution opportunity. If the team in India could produce equal or better performance than in the United States, at a lower cost, it would be a game changer. We wouldn't just be able to realize significant levels of collection revenues at a vastly lower cost; we also could make investments in other areas like analytics and technology.

They had made this happen in spite of our doubts and lack of technology investment. What was possible if we actually supported them?

"Is your team excited?" I asked Jay.

He laughed. "Right now India's getting no support." He paused. "In fact, I was in a meeting the other day with the Technology team to brainstorm ways to deal with our system challenges. I wanted it fixed immediately, but one key analyst said he didn't work on projects related to India. He just didn't believe in it."

I was incensed. "Who was it?" Maybe firing somebody for dissention would show how serious this was.

"It doesn't matter who." Jay thankfully waved me off. "He's just an example of what I encounter every day."

"Don't they get how important this is?"

"Absolutely, Brandon. But they also know the company is struggling and their jobs might be in jeopardy. A lot of people assume you have a plan you're not sharing."

I was getting madder by the minute. Over the last year I had gone to each department and explained Encore's challenge. The high cost-to-collect was keeping us from buying new portfolios. India was the only way to make lasting change. It was *the* critical element on our path to sustainable growth. Failure in India could mean failure in the United States. Why was this so difficult for people to understand?

"Other than that IT example," I tried to ask more calmly, "what does this lack of support look like?"

"The best way to describe it is that nothing about India is easy," Jay said. "I spend time fighting with people who believe we are prioritizing India's needs over theirs. The HR and IT departments can only focus on a limited number of challenges, so the ones in India get de-prioritized. It is death by a thousand cuts."

I thanked Jay for his candor. Over the next weeks, I asked similar questions of people all over the company, and heard similar perspectives. I began to see the situation through a new lens. India was causing friction throughout the organization. While I was frustrated by it, I realized even I had been limiting India's potential based on my beliefs. I had to find a way to turn people's attitudes around. Without that, I was pessimistic about our ability to navigate forward.

SHAYNE

After several years of working to improve Encore's culture, Brandon remarked to me, "I had no idea it was *that* bad." And make no mistake; Encore was barely average in its level of organizational dysfunction. Like many executives, Brandon hadn't realized how much time and energy were used up by posturing and squabbling. Even when executives are faced with a burning platform and are made aware of the cultural dysfunctions in their organization, they tend to underestimate the negative impact on the real-world results they deliver.

With the benefit of hindsight, CFO Paul Grinberg reflected on strategic decisions Encore made in 2005. "We spent a heck of a lot of time arguing with each other instead of figuring out how to move the organization forward. Key leaders would tell their teams not to trust the input of other departments. We lost hours of productivity. Then, in the end, we didn't pursue strategies that were very profitable for our competitors, and we didn't optimize the ones we did choose."

It's impossible to know if they would have made the "right" decisions had they communicated more effectively. What we do know, however, is that ineffective conversations almost always lead to making the "wrong" ones. When smart people don't listen to each other, their value cancels each other out.

These ego dynamics affect an organization's most important strategies. Brandon believed that the India strategy was a question of life or death for Encore. Yet, despite broad awareness of these stakes, the initiative suffered a "death by a thousand cuts."

The cultural dysfunctions, stuck relationships, and disharmony also took a toll on Encore's financial performance in less obvious ways. While Brandon and his team could quantitatively determine the difference between a dollar collected in India and one collected in the United States, it was harder to assign a value to other missed opportunities.

At Encore, leaders in pivotal stretch roles weren't seeking help and receiving feedback. The Strategic Initiatives team was developing crucial business strategies only to have Operations discard their ideas out of hand. The tug of war between Finance and Operations led to a budget with no ownership. The new business ventures struggled due to lack of support. While the combined impact of this dysfunction was difficult to measure, Brandon realized it was significant.

Our beliefs and actions have a human cost as well. The leadership team in India felt Encore's lack of commitment, even if they didn't understand what was going on stateside. "We felt irrelevant for a long time," Manu explained. "There was no sense of what the future looked like. They gave us low-value accounts, so our collectors couldn't produce results. People here felt like they were failing, and they left. The U.S. saw our poor collections as proof that India couldn't work, so they didn't trust us with better opportunities. The attrition got higher, reconfirming for the Americans that India couldn't function. They didn't trust us, and quite frankly, I didn't trust them."

Initially, the net result was that a big, hairy, audacious challenge—opening a call center in India and completely changing the cost structure of the company—didn't even make a small dent on Encore's profit and loss statement. If it hadn't been for the commitment and personal evolution of Manu, Brandon, and others, the cycle would likely have continued until they gave up. As higher-quality accounts were shared more broadly with the Indian workforce, and the Us vs. Them dynamics were addressed, this would change.

No organization can be completely "ego-free," and many succeed despite whatever individual and cultural egosystem dysfunctions they exhibit. Encore had many of these same issues in 2004, but favorable industry conditions helped them get away with it in the short term. By 2007, however, if Brandon couldn't lead his organization to earnestly and energetically work as one to achieve their most important strategies, he feared Encore's very survival was at stake.

What are these egosystem tendencies in your organization? How do they disrupt your pivotal operations and most critical strategies? What is the cost to you of underachieving in this way? History indicates that it's not wise to wait until a burning platform forces you to examine these questions; almost 90 percent of Fortune 500 companies in 1955 were gone by 2014. Doing the work when conditions are favorable builds a foundation for when they are not.

THE DOLLAR COST OF THE EGOSYSTEM

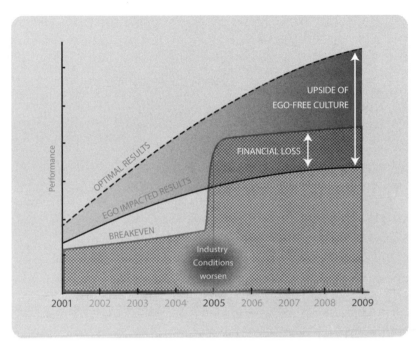

Egosystem dynamics (e.g., lack of individual growth and accountability, self-fulfilling prophecies, Us vs. Them dynamics) directly affect operational performance. Needed collaboration doesn't occur or groups actually undermine each other. The dollar value of these poorer results is defined by what is at stake in a given initiative or organization. The difference to Encore of India succeeding or failing would prove to be $90 million *per year*.

Even more than avoiding an unwanted downside, what is the opportunity cost to your organization of departments working against each other or deflecting responsibility? If you dissolved these energy quagmires, what untapped capacity might you leverage for a new kind of result?

Little did Brandon suspect that transforming these dynamics would add tens of millions of dollars a year to Encore's bottom line.

CHAPTER 4

STOP PRETENDING YOU'RE NOT VULNERABLE

The Importance of Emotional Safety

BRANDON

Our cantankerous reforecast process confirmed my worst fears. Profitability for the upcoming year—2008—was going to be down significantly unless we made meaningful cost reductions. Encore is a people business, with salaries and benefits being the most significant expense. Sadly, cost reduction meant eliminating people, and we needed to reduce headcount by 10 percent. Given the deep divisions between our corporate teams, and the unhealthy competition between the domestic and Indian operations, getting everybody on the same page was going to be difficult. I was worried about the impact a layoff would have on morale and performance.

I sat down with the leadership team to outline a process for making the personnel decisions. For me, this wasn't a numbers exercise. I knew our employees well; many of them had been there for a long time and had made sacrifices for the company. They trusted me, and I felt I was personally letting them down. My team and I had a long talk, and surprisingly, there was no pointing of fingers or posturing. Several executives had been through layoffs at other companies where the process had been cold and calculated, so we decided to create a process focused on empathy. Each individual agreed to do whatever it took to ensure that every affected employee would receive the support he or she needed to make the transition. After the meeting, several executives came up to me individually and thanked me for making the employees our priority.

Nonetheless, it was a sobering moment for me. We were going to terminate over a hundred people, and I couldn't help wondering how much my conflict avoidance and our ineffective cross-department collaboration had contributed to the poor performance making this layoff a necessity.

Despite the team's good intentions, Paul and I were concerned about a leak. We didn't have final approval from our board and couldn't afford to have the workforce find out in advance. We decided that the executive team would be the only individuals informed of the situation. We gave each of them a target and asked them to recommend specific individuals to eliminate. One senior leader, however, didn't feel close to the people several layers down and felt uncomfortable making decisions without input from his managers. He asked if he could talk to a few of his direct reports in confidence. I thought the request was reasonable and consulted with Paul about expanding the universe of people in the know.

"Have you lost your mind?" Paul objected. "You know this place.

Everybody is scheming to get information through back channels. Just the other day, somebody was in my office telling me the Operations team was snooping around trying to find out our results for the quarter. Involving more people will be a disaster."

On one hand, Paul was right: My extended leadership team seemed to have an insatiable appetite for gossip. As the CEO of a public company, I needed to ensure that material information was disseminated to our shareholders in a timely fashion and communicated through proper channels. A reduction of employees warranted public disclosure. On the other hand, how could we make the right decisions about whom to lay off without input from direct managers? This confidentiality issue had come up often, with my team criticizing me for keeping important items secret and reinforcing an in-group/out-group dynamic.

Whichever decision I made, it would fall on me if it backfired. When I talked with Dana and Shayne about my worries, they both asked similar questions. Why didn't I think I could trust the broader team? What had caused previous leaks and why did I think it would happen again? Did I worry about specific people, or was it a blanket fear? When I really thought about it, much of the historical gossip at Encore was just different departments jockeying for the upper hand. Many of these leaders were now part of WeLead and were aware of our goal of eliminating silos. I knew they were feeling more invested in the company as a whole. Had they changed enough for me to trust them? Was it arrogant of me to think Paul and I had a gene that others didn't that allowed us to keep secrets?

Reviewing the four cultural goals of WeLead pushed me to ask myself another question: How could I expect to build a culture of co-responsibility when I wasn't willing to involve people in critical decisions?

One of the cost-reduction recommendations was to eliminate the team focused on acquiring healthcare receivables. What had seemed like a natural transition in 2005 ended up being much more challenging, with returns that didn't justify continued investment. I needed to tell one of my direct reports, Fritz, that he was being let go. Several times during his tenure at Encore we had talked about his not wanting to let me down. As his division's financial struggles continued, this outcome had become increasingly more likely. Instead of facing reality, however, I had begun to avoid him.

Fritz had given me a call a few days prior to my discussion with Paul about including a broader audience to ask if there were any pending decisions about the Healthcare division. On impulse, I told him no. Upon reflection, though, I decided it was time for me to start being transparent with him.

Fritz and I met for lunch at a local Chinese restaurant. I wanted to connect with him as a person instead of treating him as an issue to check off my list. After a few minutes of small talk, I told him, "When you called me the other day, I lied to you. I wasn't prepared for the conversation." I expected him to be angry.

After a pause, however, he said, "I appreciate you being honest with me. I guess that means you're shutting our business down?"

"It does." It was a relief to have it on the table.

"I'm not surprised," he said with a sigh. "OK, let's talk about what needs to happen. I'll do whatever it takes to help my folks transition safely."

I stared at him. He had just found out he was losing his job, yet he was professional enough to stay focused on our overall goals for the lay-off. He expressed his desire to tell his team personally and to unwind the business in a way that lived up to the promises he had made to partners. At the end of the meeting, we shook hands. It was our first authentic conversation in a long time, if not ever.

The meeting with Fritz settled the issue of inclusivity in my mind.

The organization would benefit from having more people involved. The risk of not expanding the universe was too great. We quickly set up an off-site meeting with a broad set of managers to surface questions and develop a timeline for the changes.

Logistically, the meeting was a challenge because we were planning layoffs at multiple sites: our headquarters in San Diego and our operating sites in Phoenix, Arizona, and Arlington, Texas. While no reductions were planned for our other sites in St. Cloud, Minnesota, and New Delhi, India, we included them as well. To avoid raising suspicions, we sent everyone an invitation to attend a strategy session in early September.

The fifty or so people in the conference room were in a good mood as I walked in. Normally, I would go around welcoming folks, but not this time. I was nervous about my ability to pull the team together and wanted to get started as soon as possible.

"This is one of the most important meetings you'll attend at Encore," I told them, "but unfortunately, it's not the kind you were expecting. We're not here to talk about growth strategies. We're facing a very challenging situation, and each of you plays a pivotal role in its success. We need to let go of 110 employees, and we're shutting down our Healthcare division."

In the quiet of the room, everybody's eyes shifted to Fritz, seated beside me.

"Brandon and I have talked," Fritz told them, "so I knew this was coming. What's important right now is pulling together to make sure this goes well. It won't be easy for anyone."

I was grateful for Fritz's words and saw how important they were for everyone. If a guy who was losing his job could focus on taking care of the larger challenge, without blaming the company, so could they.

"I have never led a team through anything like this," I said, "and I'm a little overwhelmed by the challenge. I need all of you to help me. There is no way we will succeed unless we work together.

"Everything is likely to happen in the next week," I concluded. "Pending approval from the board, we're going to plan on letting the affected employees know first thing Monday, September 17. Until then, everything needs to be confidential."

I looked around the room trying to gauge their reliability. The group looked back at me. How we did this would significantly affect whether we built our culture on a foundation of trust or cynicism. Everybody seemed to appreciate that.

SHAYNE

It can be easy to judge the insufficient communication between Fritz and Brandon—of course they should have been talking—or to reproach Brandon for not giving Dave performance feedback more frequently. The *theoretical* importance of having authentic, transparent conversations isn't in question; it's rather the *practical difficulty of doing so when there isn't emotional safety in the relationship.*

"Safety" can be defined in many ways, like job security, work site safety, or financial well-being. But the critical importance of "emotional safety" is often ignored at great cost. It is the foundation of a healthy and productive organizational culture and *allows all other positive cultural attributes to flourish.* If people feel supported and respected in a context of trust, they can face any difficulty, including losing their livelihood. If people feel in danger—even if their job is guaranteed for life—they invariably react to protect themselves.

A lack of emotional safety in a relationship or team comes in many forms: feeling judged, blamed, or disrespected; perceiving that others are dishonest, talking behind our back, or withholding important information; feeling competitive or unsupported. It's the experience of needing to watch out, that others are a threat to our success or self-image. Feeling unsafe leads to feelings of stress and to reactions of avoidance or aggression.

Unfortunately, many of today's organizations actually encourage fear, dysfunction, and misalignment because of how they go about managing performance. The prevailing thinking seems to be that if people are measured and rewarded in competition with each other, they will work harder and produce more. While this may be true for a subset of people, it is not sustainable or inspiring, nor is it true on a team or interdepartmental level. When leaders feel unsafe—about job security, others' judgments, how trustworthy or transparent management is—*they will act to protect themselves first, do their job second, and pursue the organization's mission last.* This isn't just a problem for lower-level employees; it is true right up through the C-suite.

A common trap in creating emotional safety is to wait for our colleagues to be trustworthy before we trust them enough to be authentic. Counter-intuitively, trust and emotional safety work the other way: In taking the risk of authentically disclosing our difficulties, we make it safe for others to follow suit. The result is the creation of trust.

The breakdown between Brandon and Fritz illustrates the danger of playing the "you first" waiting game. Once they got off track, the lack of safety both men felt with each other made it too risky to talk about the performance shortfall in Healthcare, causing their frustrations and judgments to build up. This continued until Brandon disclosed something quite vulnerable: He had lied to Fritz and had done so because he was afraid to tell him that his division was closing. "It would have been much easier to just tell Fritz he was gone," Brandon said.

Instead . . .

"In my two years at Encore," Fritz recalled, "I felt closest to Brandon when he admitted he lied to me."

As unlikely as it seems, this type of response to vulnerability is consistently the case. Instead of protecting his image of being a smart and competent CEO, Brandon was determined to connect with Fritz as a person, and he owned up to his imperfection and frailty. This act of human vulnerability—which felt scary—allowed Fritz to see behind Brandon's desired image and, consequently, to feel safer. Fritz's attention shifted from how Brandon was unfairly judging him to how Brandon was struggling and in need of help. This is emblematic of the unexpected power of being vulnerable and real—which doesn't happen when we are promoting or defending our desired and dreaded images.

"There were a lot of ways Brandon could have approached that," Fritz said. "Dishonest; too cute by half. He was straight up honest. If we had talked that way before, it wouldn't have changed the business facts, but it would have helped. As it was, it enhanced my desire to support the transition. I could see he was in a tough place."

Their newfound alignment made a difference, and it set a tone of enterprise leadership throughout the layoffs. Fritz's behavior helped give Brandon confidence that he could trust a broad team of leaders with this important secret. Instead of looking for reasons not to share, he openly talked about his fears. That group included Kasey, who had just joined Encore as a senior manager in the Human Resources department. One of her first priorities was to manage all the details of the layoff. "I had second thoughts about joining Encore after hearing about the layoff," Kasey recalled. "But after a few meetings with the leadership team, I could see that everybody cared so much about the people impacted. It made me fully committed to the company."

The Power of Vulnerability and Empathy

BRANDON

The next week was a long one. Understandably, when you hear about a company doing a layoff, there is little talk of the emotional toll it takes on the people carrying it out. As human beings, however, the last thing we want to do is hurt others. The impacted employees have bills to pay and families to support; most of them are committed to the success of the company and feel shocked by a transition they are not choosing. I felt that each member of the team assigned to work on the project was deeply aware of this.

We met with our board on Friday morning to review the final plan. Their approval made the proposed changes official. We had forty-eight hours to sleep on it and finalize any remaining details.

I wanted the notifications to affected employees and the subsequent broader announcements to be sincere and contrite. The departing employees needed to walk out with their heads high, knowing they weren't being abandoned by the organization. I asked the leadership team to be accessible for every question that came up—and to be patient when people got angry or cried. An executive went to each site, and I stayed in San Diego to address employees and answer any shareholder questions. The largest headcount reduction would occur in Phoenix, so our SVP of Operations, Jim Syran, went to personally deliver the message.

I woke up early Monday morning after a poor night's sleep. I had practiced my speech over and over again in my head and felt prepared. When I arrived at work, lights were on in the offices of the HR team, who had been there since 6:00 am preparing for the day. As I approached my office, I saw an employee whose name was on "the list." For the past week, I had been interacting seamlessly with people I knew would be terminated. Somehow I had been able to compartmentalize this moment.

Today was different. I was hit by a wave of emotion and walked directly into my office without acknowledging him. I felt sick to my stomach.

The plan was to have each impacted individual privately meet with his or her manager before we held a company-wide meeting. After the first few meetings, however, the employees knew something was up. I could hear chatter, but when I walked out of my office, everybody fell silent. When I turned around, the talking resumed. Most of them had nothing to worry about, but I couldn't tell them that. I felt helpless.

Several employees being let go had been with the company for a long time, and I wanted to talk with them personally. I walked into one of these meetings and found the person in tears. I didn't know what to say, so I sat down beside her.

"How are you doing?" I finally asked. It felt like a stupid question.

She turned and looked at me. "Thank you," she said.

Am I in the wrong meeting?

"I really appreciate that you cared enough to come see me," she told me.

It was an act of grace.

I left the conference room determined not to have to make a decision like this again. I saw how my fears and avoidance had caused problems to pile up. The employees needed me to figure out a way to grow the organization successfully while maintaining cost discipline—*no matter how uncomfortable it was for my ego*. I committed in that moment to do whatever it took to live up to that responsibility.

I had a call at noon with leaders at each site to get a progress report. Things went as well as could be expected, especially in Phoenix, where about 33 percent of the employees were being let go. Jim had done an amazing job of delivering a message that didn't come across as scripted or distant. Instead of blaming the change on industry challenges or a corporate mandate, he took ownership for the decision. He addressed the entire site and answered all their questions. Initially, people were angry and didn't want to see their friends go. They saw this as the first step toward closing the site. Instead of being defensive, he empathized with their perspective and emotions. More unnerving, he walked around the call center floor, talking to people as they packed up. Nobody liked the message, but they appreciated his willingness to be there with them. By the time he'd left, the emotion had subsided greatly.

We debriefed with our outplacement firm Lee Hecht Harrison afterward to get their assessment. They told Sharon it was "one of the best layoffs they had ever seen." It wasn't something I would put on my resume, but I was proud of everyone involved, both those who stayed and those who departed.

SHAYNE

"I was very uncomfortable walking the floor after the announcement," Jim Syran said. "A lot of employees were quite upset. People's moms and sons were being laid off. I had no clue what to say or do."

Jim was facing a highly emotional situation. He worried he was harming people and feared their anger, blame, or tears. He felt overwhelmed and ill equipped. He, like many of the employees packing their belongings, felt vulnerable.

"Feeling vulnerable" is the primal sensation of facing a potential physical or emotional danger. In modern times, that usually means the risk of judgment, failure, embarrassment, or rejection. I want to acknowledge the strong intensity of this discomfort—it can feel life threatening, which is why we spend so much energy avoiding it—while reminding us that the potential consequences are mainly discomfort to our ego.

Layoffs, performance reviews, and interpersonal conflicts are common workplace events that can make both implementers and recipients feel quite vulnerable. When leaders in positions of authority don't work through their egosystems' threats in these moments, they fall into fairly predictable fight–flight behaviors. Avoiding others, becoming harsh, and relying on rationalizations all help numb the pain of the event and remove any blame we feel.

"I had a call with my LaL coach, Marc-André Olivier, the morning of the layoff," Jim recalled. "I walked him through my presentation. I had the math, the rationale. I had scripted out the business case. As Marc-André probed me to see how I was feeling, it became apparent that I was focused on protecting how I appeared.

"All these people reported to me, and I was overseeing their terminations. I didn't want them to think I was wrong or thoughtless or that I didn't care. I didn't want to be a bad person in their eyes. So I had unconsciously slanted my slides to prove it wasn't my fault. That it was the right decision and I had to do it. I wasn't thinking about what they needed in that moment."

Jim's presentation would have been professional and logical, but its overriding, unconscious intent would have been to prove he was irreproachable. Even if he delivered a flawless message, his workforce would have sensed he was shifting the burden. That he wasn't really emotionally present for their pain.

Although understandable, these self-protective reactions tend to aggravate already difficult situations. Losing our livelihood against our will is scary. If our previous colleagues are withdrawn or harsh, it adds an element of abandonment, humiliation, and a lost sense of belonging. These intangibles can be as painful as the financial hardship.

Jim, Brandon, and the rest of Encore's leadership team were able to empathize more profoundly with the people losing their jobs because they were aware of their own vulnerability as leaders. Brandon could have rationalized the layoff as life in corporate America. Instead, he let himself feel the human costs. He sat beside the long-term employee losing her job. In being more in touch with our own feelings, we are better able to empathize with others, and more inspired to take them into account.

Empathy is not sympathy, which is the act of sharing the feelings of another person, especially sorrow or difficulty. Sympathy can often lead us to rationalize someone's shortcomings or try to fix a situation. In an organizational perspective, this can contribute to inaction—for example, on performance issues. Empathy is the ability to understand another person's feelings and perspective; to put ourselves in their shoes and sense that we could feel the way they do. Used properly, empathy not only influences how we have a difficult conversation or make a hard decision, it also enables us to even do it at all.

Coming out of his coaching call, Jim turned his attention to what his people, rather than his ego, needed. Reconnected with his goal to create an atmosphere of dignity and humanity, Jim focused on ensuring that people understood clearly what was going on and letting them know he was there to emotionally support them.

"I was able to be present in a completely different way," he described. "I decided that no matter how uncomfortable I felt, I would show up for them. I felt really vulnerable."

The lesson here isn't to do this or that strategy, like walk the floor. In fact, Jim had no idea what to do. Just as Brandon felt stupid for asking his long-time employee how she was, Jim felt incompetent that morning. And yet it was a day in his career where he made a great difference for his employees. "People came up to me afterward," Jim said, "and thanked me for staying there. For not being the executive who delivers the message and then disappears." In setting aside his self-worth preoccupation, he stepped into what the situation needed.

In today's tumultuous global economy, it is impossible for companies to guarantee employment, much less assure employees that they will always get a raise or only receive positive performance feedback. These moments of vulnerability *will* happen. What matters most is how leadership behaves during these difficulties. Encore's employees saw that even when the worst occurred, leadership would be "in it together" with them.

"Odd as it sounds," Fritz said years later as a successful CEO in Southern California, "I treasure my couple of years at Encore, including how it ended. Firing someone can be traumatic for their personal life, their finances, their ego. That experience has made me more caring and thoughtful when I need to make those decisions."

How to Create a Safe Space

BRANDON

We didn't see many prolonged effects from the layoffs. To the contrary, we had no incremental attrition, and employee engagement surveys indicated morale was higher than it had been in years. That was the good news. The bad news was that portfolio pricing continued at unsustainable levels and our stock price was down significantly. As a team we had pulled together beautifully around the personnel reductions, but I worried that the external pressures on the business would undo our positive momentum.

In addition, a doubt still persisted in the organization as to whether the layoff was really about moving jobs from the United States to India, where no job reductions occurred. The word "outsourcing" was everywhere in the news, and companies were often viewed as anti-American if they moved jobs offshore. But India was one of our two strategic imperatives, and we needed to do everything we could to make it successful.

One of my key forums for communication was an all-employee meeting after each earnings release to provide context about our results and answer any questions. The November 2007 meeting was the first since the layoff. I knew there had to be some lingering questions and I wanted to make sure they had the chance to hear the answers from me.

We gathered the San Diego employees in a conference room late on a Tuesday afternoon. From collectors to statisticians to software engineers, we employed a diverse array of individuals at our headquarters, and I was addressing people from every department. I spent thirty minutes explaining the results using a PowerPoint presentation and then opened up the floor to questions. A minute went by in complete silence. Trying to break the ice, I assured them I wasn't going to let them go until I got at least one question.

"Why aren't you telling us when you're closing the site and moving our jobs to India?" asked Jonathan, one of the most tenured account managers in the company. He had a forceful presence and his voice was deep and commanding. It was a statement, not a question.

I was pissed. I had worked with Jonathan for almost a decade. *You should trust my motives by now!* I almost growled back. I felt he was challenging my moral compass.

I took a deep breath, realizing I'd had a pinch.

"Great question," I said, trying to buy some time. I'd known this was coming—I just didn't expect it to be this direct a challenge. "I'm sure this is on many people's minds, so thank you for bringing it up."

"So are you going to tell us when our jobs are moving to India?"

"They're not."

"Not today, or not ever?"

My ears were hot, and I felt adrenalin pumping through my body. *Take a moment,* I instructed myself. *What's my ego threat?* Several jumped out immediately: that he was accusing me of being dishonest and selfish, and that I looked like a bad leader. *So if that's just my ego, what's truly important right now?*

I'd told my team that answering questions about our plans for India would be pivotal if we were to gain the trust of the employees. This was that moment. If I debated him or shut him down, we'd take a big step backward.

As a leader, you are cautioned to "never say 'never.'" Any future decision that contradicted what I said now would likely be held over my head as proof I was untrustworthy. Saying "never" here seemed foolhardy; if India's performance consistently rivaled that of our domestic workforce, moving jobs overseas would become very financially compelling. My responsibility was to maximize returns for our shareholders; how could I justify *not* taking advantage of this lower-cost environment?

"Let's focus on why jobs are not moving, but without the ultimatums." I tried to de-escalate the tone. There was chatter in the room. *What do they need right now?* "Let's talk about what this would mean to all of you if I made that decision."

"It would certainly mean a lot more to me than to you," Jonathan said. He was still angry. "You would keep your job."

I felt another pinch, but not as strong. *They're afraid.* Jonathan and the other employees needed to know I understood the potential impact on him and the people in the room from an *emotional* perspective, not an analytical one.

"You're right," I said. "If I did what you fear, it would impact you more than me. I take that very seriously. Now, let me tell you what I fear. I see how we are struggling to really commit to our India strategy: the communication breakdowns and the hallway griping about the time difference. If you believe that I'm going to ship your job overseas as soon as they perform well enough, why would you want to go the extra mile to make them better?"

There was nodding in the room, and I sensed that we'd gotten their big concern out in the open. My earlier aggravation dissipated as I both empathized with their fears and saw clearly our path forward. I felt light inside.

"I worry that we won't do everything in our power to make India successful," I told them. "Because unlike what you read in the papers or see on the news, in our business, having a greater presence in India will protect jobs in the U.S., not threaten them."

"I don't understand," somebody called out.

"Very simply, if we can't bring down our costs, we won't be able to acquire new portfolios. You've all seen how difficult the last few years have been. Without new portfolios, we'll end up having more episodes like September. I don't want that, and neither do you. The only initiative that will allow us enough cost savings to be competitive is India."

Many in the room seemed to be cautiously accepting the message. I looked at Jonathan, and he nodded. The India vs. United States job equation was more complicated than a simple numbers game. If I did move jobs overseas, the true cost to productivity of a lot of turmoil might outweigh the potential labor savings. In that moment, I decided that having my employees feel safe was just as important.

"I appreciate that you're scared, but if we can all get behind this strategy, we can create something enduring at Encore. We've never eliminated a job in the United States and moved it to India, and we won't do it as long as I'm CEO."

I'm not sure they believed the last sentence, but I did. The tension had dropped in the room, and I sensed the group understood why this was important for their long-term success, not just for Encore's. I just hoped we had enough time to make the strategy work.

SHAYNE

Creating emotional safety in a team atmosphere is one of a leader's most important responsibilities. When individuals feel safe, their egosystems get deactivated; this gives team members additional brain space and fortitude to learn new skills or tackle daunting endeavors. When team members stop seeing others as a threat, they can listen, learn, and collaborate in more effective ways. A company's or a group's collective goals, instead of their ego survival, become their focal point.

In the time we had worked together, Brandon had implemented several key aspects of creating emotional safety.

1. **Eliminate seemingly innocuous but detrimental daily behaviors**. Brandon and Encore's executive team started by addressing the corrosive effects of sarcasm. It had carried a subtext of judgment and put everyone on edge, ready to counter with his or her own rejoinder. No one really knew where he or she stood.

   Most of us have a few socially acceptable habits that protect us at the expense of the quality of our relationships: being cold or reserved; checking email on our smartphone when someone is talking; being abrupt; planning what we will say next instead of listening; using extreme or dramatic language; overreacting to small things. Anything that indirectly communicates our judgments directly undermines emotional safety. Encore's commitment to stop all sarcasm dramatically cleared up this background of confusion.

   "When I first joined the company, Brandon was sarcastic," recalled SVP of Operations Jim Syran. "Not in a mean way, but if he was uncomfortable or wanted to get a message across, it came with a bite. Everyone was trying to read into what he was saying and taking things differently. He completely stopped that. It was powerful, and it changed how we interacted. We became more collaborative and honest."

2. **Address issues openly, without judgment.** Brandon's conflict avoidance with Dave and Fritz illustrates one of the most common leadership dysfunctions within large organizations. This habit undermines emotional safety on multiple levels: When a leader leaves a performance issue unaddressed, others on the team see it and get frustrated; the team member in question likely knows he or she is struggling, and is inwardly uncomfortable and on guard; as the supervisor avoiding the conversation, our frustration and judgments with the issue build, creating a self-fulfilling prophecy. Leaders who are abrasively blunt are dysfunctional in a different way. They typically express judgmental conclusions, not useful observations. Trust is lost, and employees try to hide their weaknesses. Abrasive or harsh communication is similarly triggered by fear and leads to equally strained and unsafe relationships.

Brandon combined breaking through his self-protective fears with separating his observations from his judgments. Over time, he enhanced his ability to hold up a mirror to his team while still having their backs.

3. **Grow more comfortable with being vulnerable.** Our direct reports will only be as vulnerable and transparent as we are: sometimes less so, but rarely more. As CEO, Brandon needed to find the courage both to acknowledge his shortcomings and struggles and to willingly share these difficulties with his team. He overcame the desired and dreaded images that make it so difficult for most leaders to model authenticity that starts at the top.

The more Brandon accepted his own vulnerability, the more his humility allowed him to . . .

4. **Empathize with others, even when your egosystem is triggered.**
People in our organizations experience fear every day: of failing, losing control, not being good enough, being judged, losing their jobs.
Ignoring or judging these fears, or telling people they shouldn't have
them, actually hampers their progress because they become focused
on defending themselves instead of facing their difficulty. (This is
equally true with our children.) When we empathize with others,
we give them the space to face their fears and take ownership of
their fate.

As with many aspects of working on our egosystem, the challenge
lies more in the application than in the theory. In a very public way,
Brandon encountered the first barrier to empathizing with a scared workforce: People usually don't express their fears rationally and consciously.

In the town hall meeting Jonathan said, "Why aren't you telling
us when you're closing the site and moving our jobs to India?" not
"Brandon, I fear our jobs will all be outsourced to India and I'll end
up unemployed." Jonathan was angry; anger is a less vulnerable emotion than either fear or weakness, and it frequently covers those more
primary and raw emotions. Blaming, shutting down, becoming passive-
aggressive, and lashing out are common symptoms of unexpressed fear.

In recognizing and moving beyond his own pinches, Brandon was
able to grasp with empathy what was going on for Jonathan and other
people in the room. He made it legitimate to feel trepidation, which
allowed the employees to not feel judged by the most powerful person
in the company. Only then were they able to earnestly listen.

In the end, Brandon's explanation of India's importance was similar
to what he might have said had he debated Jonathan. But the tone and
context of his message were completely different, allowing the employees to hear it as inspiring guidance rather than a scolding.

And once wasn't enough. Brandon's exchange in that quarterly meeting was just one of many about India over the course of several years.

The egosystem shines a light on the invisible ways in which we (individuals, teams, entire organizations) are *often not truly committed* to our most important endeavors. Not because we don't want them, but because our self-worth is threatened in some way. If this fear stays unconscious, unexpressed, and unaddressed, it will drive behavior more powerfully than any strategic plan on a PowerPoint. And no matter how brilliant a strategy, if the people aren't committed, it will never take off.

Note that empathizing didn't mean that Brandon didn't challenge his workforce. In fact, it actually gave him the possibility of challenging them more. Feeling unsafe is the fear of being criticized, ridiculed, or devalued. Feeling challenged, on the other hand, occurs when we are pushed to tackle a complex situation, develop a new skill, or work toward a next level. Encore needed its American employees to see beyond their current worldview and buy into Brandon's larger perspective. They were being uncomfortably challenged to perform in areas where they were not yet competent. To efficiently rise to that challenge, they needed to feel safe enough to risk failure.

As India's performance improved, many people in the coming years would pressure Brandon to revoke his commitment to not replace U.S. jobs with Indian ones. Although it appeared to be a no-brainer when they crunched the numbers, he insisted it was too narrow a view. "I had discovered just how distracting it was for people to be afraid," he explained. "If I shut down our Phoenix call center, people in our St. Cloud call center, or in Accounting or IT, wouldn't have believed me when I said their jobs were still safe. They would have doubted my intentions or worried about what was going to happen. The cultural damage wasn't worth it."

"Safety" sounds like a soft word, but as soon as it breaks down in a company, engagement levels drop and backstabbing and fiefdoms flare up. People look out for themselves. In the coming years, Encore would uncover deep financial value in their lack of drama. As Brandon put it, "The more we got people's real concerns on the table, the less we got spun up in personality conflicts. We didn't have any dissension, so we went very hard, very fast, for a long time."

BRANDON

As 2007 wound down, I made the decision to make Manu Rikhye the general manager of the India operation. Only in his early thirties, he had an amazing ability to lead people and had held the site together during this period of turmoil and underperformance.

Personally, Dana and I were getting ready for the birth of our daughter, Leah. She was due in late February and I decided to paint her room and put chair molding around the perimeter. It seemed like something a dad should do. With everything going on at work, however, I finished it at the last minute thanks to a lot of caulk and a tolerant wife. Leah was the first girl to be born on my father's side of the family in four generations.

This time of great personal celebration was a welcome distraction from the pressure I felt to produce returns at Encore. Our 2007 fourth quarter results showed year-over-year declines in collections, revenues, and profitability. By March 2008, the stock price dropped below $7, a 60 percent decrease since my promotion to CEO. Our investor relations approach was limited to talking about our past results and not speculating about the future. This didn't sit well with the growing number of disappointed shareholders asking us to "give them some hope." I could empathize; I was just barely clinging to mine.

CHAPTER 5

YOU'RE NOT REALLY LISTENING, ARE YOU?

———

The Toxic Habit of Being Right

BRANDON

"How was this morning's meeting?" I asked Shayne as we sat down for lunch in early January 2008. He had spent the first half of the day with a dozen of Encore's senior leaders. They were taking stock of interdepartmental collaboration, including the United States and India dynamic.

"Productive," he responded. "Although, toward the end, they began talking about how the priorities aren't clear. Some people aren't sure what they should be doing, or how to makes choices about what's most important."

"You were talking about *what*!?" I felt my face getting hot.

"Lack of—" Shayne looked up and stopped when he realized I'd heard him too well the first time.

"I've been hearing about this for weeks," I leaned forward. "It's nonsense. Not six weeks ago, Paul and I had a meeting with all the executives. We went through the priorities in detail. It was two hours long; everybody was present. I couldn't have been clearer." I thought about the scene in *A Few Good Men*, when Jack Nicholson asks Tom Cruise if he is being clear. "Crystal," Tom replies. That's what I had been in the meeting: crystal clear. "Two years ago I'm accused of not being open enough. Now we outline the corporate strategy in transparent, gory detail, and people don't know the priorities? That's bullshit."

"I'm not sure what to think of it," Shayne said, "but it's an issue that goes several layers down in the organization."

"There are some things I'm not great at," I told him, "but I *am* a good communicator. This is really about people not wanting to be accountable. We're still facing tough challenges, and they don't want to deal with them. It can't be their fault, so it has to be mine for not being clear. They're being morons."

He laughed. "Look at you. Something is going on. I don't understand the breakdown between you and the team, but I do recognize when you want to be right."

"No, I *am* right."

"Maybe. But you're also being judgmental and are sure of your point of view. And you've committed to not letting yourself fall into that."

"Working on myself is a good thing, but sometimes it's too much. I'm running a company here. I can't afford to have a bunch of complainers hiding behind semantics to avoid being held accountable."

Shayne sat silent as I paused to clear my head. "So, what do we do?" I finally asked.

"We're all scheduled to meet this afternoon. Let's use that forum to talk this through."

"Perfect," I told him. "It will give you a chance to see what's really going on."

I couldn't wait for the meeting. It wasn't my new-normal style, but I needed to put my foot down. If the priorities weren't clear, my feedback would be.

"I need you to put aside your frustration and really listen to them," Shayne interrupted. "Be exploratory; have a learning intention."

"Don't worry, I know that's code for 'don't be a jerk,'" I laughed. Shayne was resolute, however. He wanted me to commit to being open to their perspective. I wasn't sold, but I agreed to go into the conversation assuming there was an *actual* issue and to be open to feedback.

We went back to the office and met the team in a large, windowless conference room. Shayne briefly summarized the morning session to make sure he had correctly interpreted the group's comments. After a series of nods, he gave some guidelines and people began sharing their thoughts. To satisfy Shayne's request to be open, I decided to hear everybody out instead of responding to each person. I took notes so I could refute their points at the end.

"For me, the issue is that we don't have a way to make consistent trade-offs when priorities change," said Jay, in charge of all our call centers.

"Going into the meeting a few weeks ago, our plates were full," added another executive. "There were a ton of ongoing initiatives taking up all our time and resources. You and Paul came into the room with a list of 'new' priorities and then walked out assuming that we knew what to do with the information. Do we stop everything and start working on your new strategic priorities? We don't have a process for doing that."

"On top of it all," said another, "we are about to go through the performance review process, which will determine people's bonuses. We created goals for people back in February 2007. We are supposed to use them to determine their rating for the year. Do we let people off the hook if they didn't meet their objectives because their priorities changed?"

"Oh, and what happens when one group stops working on an initiative and another doesn't? Just yesterday, I had somebody in my office complaining that her project was stalled because her IT resources were focused on new priorities. She was pissed, and I didn't know what to tell her."

"You told us to support India, but our Technology teams are working on enabling an activity cost database, building the new legal platform, and upgrading the data center. Which one do we stop to free up the needed resources?"

The information kept flowing. I found myself writing less and listening more. We weren't having the conversation I was expecting about corporate priorities. Everybody in the room clearly understood what I had presented. They were struggling to make trade-offs between departmental objectives, legacy initiatives, and broader corporate priorities.

"OK, I hear you and what you're saying makes complete sense," I said. "Why have we been arguing about a lack of clear priorities instead of having this conversation?"

"Several of us tried to raise this issue at the end of the November meeting," replied Jim Syran, our SVP of Operations. "You told us to work together to make the appropriate trade-offs and then left the room. But who gets to decide the priorities? Can I do that or do we all have to agree? As you know, I'd be delighted to make the decisions, but my teammates probably wouldn't appreciate it. We don't know who can terminate a project and who can't."

Jim's comment hit it on the head. I hadn't appreciated the complexity left behind when we developed the list of new priorities. I thought it was going to be a natural adjustment and hadn't considered the implications for each individual and group, much less their bonuses. The last thing I wanted to do was get into people's pockets. By making all these changes right at bonus time, I had put everybody on guard.

At the conclusion of the meeting, we established a project prioritization committee and agreed that performance goals had to be dynamic. Our business was changing monthly, so we couldn't stay wedded to initiatives that could be upwards of a year old. In just over two hours, we completely cleared the air and created concrete steps for moving forward.

I had come into the meeting so certain of my perspective. What would've happened if I hadn't listened to them? It was a great learning moment for me, one I would come back to many times.

SHAYNE

For our ego, the sensation of being right is like electricity to a lightbulb. It fuels us with energy and vigor. We sit straighter, our voice sharpens, and our language hardens. We face an issue or a conflict, and we see the answer clearly. With this certainty comes a feeling of power and righteousness, as captivating as a drug rush. *This is the way it is.* Being right sweeps us so automatically into an aggressive mental stance that any collateral damage seems just a necessary evil.

In understanding how "being right" is a destructive dysfunction, it is important to separate *having a point of view* on a subject from the strong feeling that *your point of view should prevail.* Brandon's memory of how clear he and Paul had been about the corporate priorities was lucid. He wasn't completely wrong when he described his directors as complaining instead of taking responsibility. With the data he had, he *was* right. But in his agitated state of being right, he couldn't notice facets of reality he was missing—or even ask questions that might reveal them. This is particularly problematic when we hold a position of authority, because we have the power to bend other people to our will. In Brandon's case, if the directors had just shut up and gone along with him, the critical questions they raised about how they were to assimilate new priorities simply would not have been answered. And Encore's operational performance would have suffered for it.

Being right has such powerful sway over us because it plugs into our core self-worth drivers. Our egosystem *loves* the power and adrenalin of winning, knowing, and feeling superior. We are ready to argue, to take action, to throw caution to the wind.

It may come as a surprise that feeling powerful, superior, and righteous are attributes of being at the mercy. Yet, notice how we experience each of these sensations as being *over* something or someone: I am right over you; I am more powerful than this other person; I am in control of this issue or that conversation. We are the ones hung up on the issue, rehearsing arguments in our head and feeling aggravated until the other person admits he or she is wrong—and how often does that happen?! Being right is like drinking poison and hoping the other person dies.

The danger of these powerful feelings is that when we know we are right, questioning our point of view, or even incorporating other perspectives, is the *very last thing* we want to do. To Brandon, listening to his directors that afternoon initially felt like a ridiculous waste of his time. I was worried how our conversation might unfold. Arguments between people or groups who want to be right over each other almost *never* move the needle forward on the actual issue. I pushed back on Brandon during our lunch because I sensed he was agitated, the directors were sincere, and there was something we didn't yet understand.

Had Brandon been at the source at that moment, he would have been more curious: "I communicated clearly; these are intelligent, hardworking people. Something doesn't add up. What am I missing?" Having such an optimal response would seem self-evident—were it not for all the times in our own life where we don't do it.

Brandon's conscious explanation of his frustration was that he had already addressed the issue several times and that his leadership team was made up of "morons," their complaints "bullshit." At an unconscious level, however, the intensity of his reaction came from how his ego was reading between the lines of the directors' remarks. It was inferring, "You're wrong; you are a bad CEO; you are stupid and unworthy." And then Brandon's ego reacted in kind: "No, they are wrong. They are disrespecting my guidance and authority. They are the ones at fault, wasting time and resources." This triggered a fear of failure as well as a dreaded image of appearing weak or soft if he let their behavior continue.

We now begin to understand why—with the unpleasant sensations of being incompetent, failing, and appearing weak swirling inside his head—the fiery, powerful option of dismissing the directors as morons was far more exhilarating for Brandon. Like each of us, Brandon had no awareness of these underlying ego threats, but they are *always* there. Acknowledging these ego triggers gives us access to why we become *invested* in being right. They are driving the bus, and unless we identify and defuse them, we won't be able to get off.

Time and again I have seen two sides fight dogmatically over an issue. Each pointed to myriad facts that corroborated their point of view and, simultaneously, dismissed the validity of the other. *This is the way it is.* As their egos became invested in being right, they lost their ability to see that their story, though linked to facts, was no more or less true than their adversary's.

THE FALLACY OF BEING RIGHT

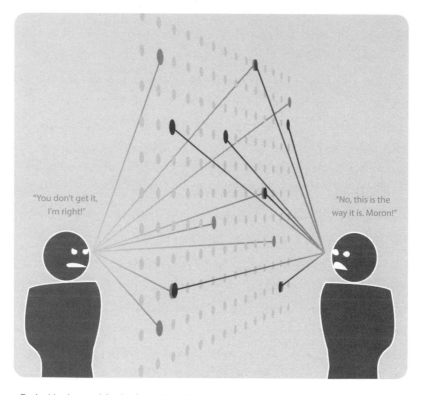

Each side cherry-picks the data points that prove their view. Sometimes these facts are the same as the other side, interpreted differently. Often they are just different facts. Other relevant facts are missed by both sides. "Being right" is a futile pursuit.

Stepping out of being right does not mean relinquishing our perspective; rather, it means surrendering our one-dimensional certainty. When we can defuse our ego threats, we regain our natural curiosity and ability to integrate multiple perspectives. The result is a greater understanding of reality, more nuanced decisions, and superior outcomes.

Reversing Downward Spirals

BRANDON

The financial results for the first half of 2008 were strong. We posted double-digit growth in collections and profits and experienced a slight decline in operating costs. Not only was the India site increasing its contribution, we were improving our understanding of which consumers would most likely repay their obligations. This increasingly allowed us to contact only those people who could pay while giving other customers time to recover. I enjoyed sharing these developments with our shareholders, who were starting to reap the benefits. The one thing that remained unchanged was the portfolio-purchasing environment. It was getting harder and harder to locate affordable new investments.

Still, the stock market responded, driving the price up from $8 per share to almost $14 by early fall. Our strong financial performance gave us the momentum to raise an additional $100 million for future portfolio purchases. Although we wouldn't need to make those purchases in the short term, our board was increasingly wary about the inflated asset prices around the globe. They wanted us to be prepared when the correction occurred.

It is amazing what a rising stock price will do for morale. Everybody was in a good mood, and the priorities discussion created a level of alignment that hadn't been in place for years. More and more leaders and teams were operating with an enterprise-wide mindset.

The past few years had seen significant turnover in my direct reports. With the departure of two executives over the summer, only Paul and Sharon remained from the original team. Getting the "right" people on the bus had taken on a new meaning—I focused on finding people with a willingness to work diligently on themselves and lead by example. It wasn't enough to be bright and experienced; they needed to fit into the new culture at Encore. In the past I had too often settled on the "best available" candidate. Going forward, I wouldn't hire somebody unless they were willing to "look in the mirror."

The company also had a new board hierarchy. George Lund was elevated to chairman in August, replacing the former CEO and my mentor, Carl Gregory. The change was significant. I had counted on Carl for guidance and I wasn't sure what to expect from George. At least it was happening while things were quiet.

It turned out to be the calm before the storm. On Monday, September 15, 2008, Lehman Brothers filed for bankruptcy and Bank of America entered into an agreement to acquire Merrill Lynch. On Tuesday, the Federal Reserve bailed out AIG, and on Wednesday, Washington Mutual announced it was for sale. These failures staggered the capital markets. It was a time of reckoning for the countless industries—including ours—that had benefited from the torrent of easy capital since 2005. The financial collapse was the catalyst that burst the inflated portfolio pricing "bubble," forcing our competitors to come to terms with years of unprofitable investments.

In the next few years, *90 percent of our industry would go out of business.*

We, meanwhile, were in the perfect position to ride the tail winds.

But the chaos and subsequent banking consolidation made it impossible to determine which companies would survive. It seemed like new governmental programs were announced daily, as the drumbeat of discord with the banks got louder and louder. Within a month most financial institutions had lost 50 percent of their market value and were being charged with causing one of the greatest financial crises in history. Acquisitions and consolidations were draining resources, diverting them away from business as usual. We had no idea if the banks would continue selling receivables; it certainly wasn't their biggest problem.

Our calls went unanswered for weeks. Despite having made all the right decisions—staying disciplined, raising capital, and investing in long-term capacity—we were sucked into the vortex of the tornado.

The market decline completely erased all of Encore's positive stock gains from earlier in the year. Stock analysts and Encore shareholders concluded that our customers—the individuals we collected money from—would be most impacted by the recession, significantly reducing Encore's revenues. These conclusions were based on speculation, and we had plenty of evidence to the contrary. But facts didn't carry the day; there was simply too much fear and distrust in the system.

Chaos also returned to the company. We were at the one-year anniversary of the layoff, and the morale boost from our rising stock price had dissipated. Employees read reports predicting the demise of our industry and feared for their jobs. On top of that, many were coping with significant losses in their personal financial accounts. I could feel their stress and anxiety all around the office. It was disheartening how quickly we fell into blaming each other again rather than solving problems. The Operations teams criticized the Business Development team for not finding portfolios to buy. The Finance department accused the Decision Science team of producing inaccurate models. It was déjà vu.

The difference, however, was how quickly we recognized the return of those dynamics. "Hey," I heard more than once, "we're in an Us vs. Them. We need to get in a room and work this out." The team began making adjustments. Every day, folks across the organization recommitted to maintaining a positive, productive working environment despite what was happening in the macro-economy.

Wanting to find a way to accelerate the learning process, I talked with Shayne about having our leadership team attend LaL's seminar in November. Initially, I was hesitant. Who sends a leadership team off for five days in the middle of a crisis? But then I thought back to when

Encore's ownership structure changed and how pivotal our team cohesion had been. Nothing was going to happen in a week that would be more lasting than investing in each other and the team.

They returned energized and much clearer about what was holding us back. Their main point of conflict during the week had been who held responsibility for two strategic mistakes in the past years: the failure of the healthcare receivables vertical and the underperformance of the 2005 acquisition. If we couldn't learn from past errors, they told me, how could we be sure we were making the best decisions now?

If there was one place we needed to be able to analyze past failures, it was in our Investment Committee, where all new investment decisions were made. The IC comprised Paul, Amy Anuk, our director of Business Development, members of our Decision Science team, the leaders of the operating units, and me. The goal of such broad representation was to guarantee that we got everybody's perspective.

The discussions in the LaL seminar, however, brought to the surface the cumulative toll that losing so many deals had taken on the people in the room. The Business Development team was tired of our conservative bidding. Several major banks had told them Encore wasn't a serious buyer and, at one point, had threatened to exclude us from bidding. The valuation team was defensive about being labeled as too conservative, and the Operations team bristled every time they were asked to step up their performance. Too often, our conversations ended in an "agree to disagree" stalemate that I needed to arbitrate. We weren't really aligned, and "I told you so" seemed to be on the tip of nearly everyone's tongue.

I felt a sense of urgency to work through these issues. The banks had begun returning our calls and we anticipated seeing a large number of new opportunities. Given the massive reduction in competition, portfolio pricing was going to decline precipitously. If we got it right, the results would be spectacular. If we stayed locked in an Us vs. Them, we ran the risk of missing our window.

Shayne and I set up a meeting with the committee members in early December 2008. The IC had two general factions—people responsible for valuing and collecting on portfolios, and the Business Development team plus Paul and me—so we divided into groups along those lines. Shayne led us through a process designed to map out the dynamic, and we identified the judgments each group had of the other. It was remarkable how otherwise sensitive comments became easier to say when we worked together to list them instead of directing them at each other.

This is how the valuation team saw us:

1. Not being concerned enough about emerging trends and relying too often on dated information

2. Overly simplifying the operational complexity of some deals

3. Rejecting data that didn't fit our hypothesis

4. Having a selective memory—only recalling the deals that did well and forgetting the ones that failed

5. Being overly optimistic

On the other hand, this is how we saw them:

1. Making things overly complex to avoid doing challenging deals

2. Having the memory of elephants—only remembering the deals that went wrong

3. Always being negative and quick to point out other people's mistakes

4. Unwilling to take risks, even calculated ones

We were struck by how our beliefs and frustrations were mirror images. More startling was how these judgments drove almost identical behavior: Both sides tended to disengage, to discount the impartiality of the other side, and to vent and seek alliances with others. We were inadvertently dividing the team and undermining our ability to make good decisions together. It was sand in the gears.

With prodding, we talked about how our egos were driving our respective positions. Both groups were driven to succeed—defined as "not being seen as failures." The fear of being blamed was causing the data-driven folks to play not to lose rather than strive to win. Not buying anything was more comfortable than taking calculated risks. For us, success meant "winning"—the argument in the meeting, the bid—even if the deal was unwise for the company.

Besides missing our growth and profit targets, we identified other costs for Encore if we didn't change our behaviors: the demotivation and potential loss of key members of the team; an overall deterioration in the corporate culture; and the real likelihood that the dysfunction at work would spill over into people's personal lives. The members of the IC influenced the vast majority of the employees. Our collective morale would help determine how far the company went in 2009 and beyond. Recognizing what was at stake helped us go beyond our judgments and mistrust. We made commitments to break the current paradigm and eliminate the factions. We were ready to have each other's backs and take calculated risks, knowing some deals would not be profitable. When that occurred, we would look to identify the root causes—not to point fingers but to ensure that the same mistake wouldn't happen again.

I walked out of our meeting with a feeling of accomplishment. In just one afternoon we had identified collaborative solutions for a major problem that had festered for a long time. How many other challenges could we handle this effectively if we committed to this type of open dialogue and exploration?

SHAYNE

Even when we grasp what proper collaboration looks like, if we don't recognize when our ego has been triggered during a workplace interaction, we *will* contribute to mistrust and discord through our frustration and agitation. So the first indispensable step in creating change is to sort our pinch. Then, applied earnestly and consistently, certain strategies can transform dysfunctional teams into highly productive ones.

1. **Name the dynamic together rather than blame one another.** Here are three practical ways to keep your team focused on the problem, not the imperfect people trying to solve it:

   - **Avoid inflammatory and judgmental language.** Express your observations, not your conclusions. Rather than use words like "never" or "always," or make blanket statements to emphasize your frustration, briefly, clearly state what you see. This moves the conversation away from character assassination and toward observable behavior.

   - **Describe the reinforcing communication loop you create together.** When someone simply states, "this is what is playing out between us" rather than "this is what *you* are doing to me," it helps everyone see that each side's judgments are often mirror images of the other.

   - **Recognize your impulse to be right.** Your analysis of any situation is a collage of beliefs, not fact, and is *always* incomplete and biased. By proactively questioning your conclusions, your perspective can expand to include a more accurate picture of reality.

2. **Identify your ego threats and communicate them with vulnerability.** Most of us have a major blind spot in our professional and personal relationships: Our fear of others' judgment thwarts

us from realizing that others feel just as afraid as we do. Disclosing your fears vulnerably to others shatters this facade.

Although this can feel uncomfortable, these anxieties are only potent when we keep them to ourselves. *Expressed collectively, our fears dissipate.* Time and again, I have witnessed the majority of the tension in a room vanish when a team member—particularly a leader—frankly admits his or her fear of being judged. A reinforcing cycle of mutual empathy replaces the downward spiral of mutual judgment.

3. **Acknowledge the consequences of your Us vs. Them dysfunction.** When we are caught up in our Us vs. Them dynamics, our frustrations with the other side lead us to ignore the damage *we* are causing with our gridlock and accusations. The IC team named close to thirty discrete costs, such as "missed growth/profit goals"; "make bad decisions because we're not objective"; "I don't want to work here unless this changes"; "I'm failing other people in this company by not contributing to our success." Confronting the brutal truth of their dysfunctional interactions was a rude shock. When we acknowledge, on an emotional level, the consequences of our behavior, it inspires us to challenge our certainties about the conflict.

4. **Seek to understand how you are contributing to the problem.** Another classic symptom of Us vs. Them dynamics is that we view ourselves as the well-intended, competent party and the others as the problem. This is almost universally untrue.

   Shifting these dynamics requires challenging both biases. Where is our side not as perfect as we profess? What valuable contribution and valid perspective are we dismissing from the other group? What is true about their frustrations with us? Are we blaming them for something that is a mutual or company-wide problem?

By talking openly about your biases, it becomes easier to trust another group's input as a "net balanced view'" coming from a different perspective. Of course, it works much better when both sides are committed to transparently questioning their assumptions. There are cases, however, where one side starts rebalancing and inspires the other side to do the same.

5. **Align on your collective goals.** One of the fallacies of Us vs. Them dynamics is that each side believes its goals and interests are *in competition* with the other. Seeing beyond one team's priorities and articulating common goals with an opposing group helps heighten our awareness of what is really at stake. We all have a deep desire to be connected to a larger cause, and clarifying this with others is inspiring.

The Investment Committee Us vs. Them meeting occurred almost three years into Encore's work with LaL. Why? Shouldn't they have fixed this issue in the first month?

Individual and cultural dysfunctions and discord heal in stages. Unhelpfully, people often assume that these issues will go away once we identify them. They oscillate between resignation—"these interpersonal issues are intractable"—and aggravated impatience—"these issues should be gone already; what's taking so long?" These patterns build up over decades, and it takes time to reverse them. Self-awareness and personal mastery are skill sets we build with commitment and practice.

"There was a cumulative effect of doing this work on ourselves so consistently over time," Brandon explained. "We got better at it. Initially, we couldn't even talk about issues. Then we grudgingly admitted them. Then we called them out without stigma or overreaction. By that day in the Investment Committee, we had built the emotional maturity to be direct about the dynamic and move through it."

Creating Constructive Communication

BRANDON

I finalized bonus recommendations for the leadership team and presented them to the Compensation Committee of the board in early January 2009. Although we didn't achieve all our financial goals, I believed the team deserved to be paid 100 percent of their bonuses. We had overcome many obstacles, were weathering the worst recession in decades, and had legitimate explanations for performance shortfalls. The board accepted my recommendations.

Given what they approved for my team, I assumed I would be treated similarly. They had a different perspective.

"As the CEO," a committee member told me, "it is ultimately your responsibility to ensure we achieve our financial targets and deliver returns to our shareholders. Our stock is down to $6 per share. Since we failed, your bonus should reflect that shortfall." They knew our misses had nothing to do with anything under Encore's control. It wasn't my fault the financial markets melted down and banks were temporarily paralyzed. Moreover, we had prepared for just this time. January 2009 was on track to be our highest collection month ever. I tried to understand their logic, but couldn't.

Worse, I began to recognize a troubling trend of events that started in the fourth quarter of 2008. Shortly after George replaced Carl as chairman, he held a series of meetings with select board members. I was not invited. Then, several strategic recommendations I made during board meetings weren't approved. Rather than accept my explanations, George and those select members had begun to question me in great detail about the operations of the company. In between the board meetings, I was surprised by offensively curt emails from certain board members. Now my bonus. A former boss once told me that successful executives are able to draw a curve with only a few data points. Here, I had plenty, and they were all pointing in the same direction.

Debt collection was uninspiring, my stock options were worthless, the board was meddling and incompetent—most of their ideas were off base and their scrutiny was anything but helpful—and now they weren't recognizing my worth by underpaying me. Despite all the progress we were making as a team, maybe it was time for me to move on.

Shayne and I had a coaching call scheduled for the next day. I almost canceled but decided to use him to help plan my transition. "I've had enough of this," I told him as he picked up the phone. "Too much has happened over the past six months that I can't tolerate." I gave him a quick recap of the evidence. "I think it's time for me to leave Encore."

"Whoa, I don't recall talking about any of this."

"I was too focused on doing whatever it took to navigate the financial crisis. Evidently, while I was doing that, the board was second-guessing my decisions and talking behind my back. It wasn't until my conversation around compensation that I put two and two together." I vented to Shayne about the board's focus on unimportant details, not valuing the strategies Paul and I had developed, and their inflated view of their own value.

"Slow down," he said, "what's going on?"

"Facts don't lie, Shayne. They're going to scapegoat me."

"OK," he paused, "so you're afraid."

I almost hung up the phone. Despite my anger, though, I realized his voice wasn't aggressive. As we talked more and I thought about his comment, I realized that behind my anger there *was* fear. Fear they didn't think I was the right CEO, fear of being fired. The fear that maybe I really wasn't capable. Acknowledging this was both unpleasant and somehow calming.

"You've talked in the past about regretting how you left Capital One," Shayne continued. "Didn't something similar happen there? You blamed them for doing things wrong and got so angry you left? Do you think you could be repeating the same pattern here?"

I didn't like that idea. But each angle I took came back to the same tension: I was scared they would tell me I wasn't good enough. "I think that's right," I admitted. "The more I blame the board for what's not working, the less it's my fault when I'm asked to leave." And that was exactly what happened at Capital One.

"When we leave a job," Shayne said, "or sever a relationship, we think we're escaping unwanted circumstances or people. But our internal challenge in that situation just keeps repeating itself. You will leave jobs again and again, with similar consequences, until you face this difficulty differently."

I thought about the years of heartache I felt after leaving Capital One. My departure put the company in a difficult predicament and led to a protracted lawsuit over a non-compete agreement. The situation forced my coworkers to choose between their friendship with me and their relationship with their current employer. Many distanced themselves from me, and I was hurt. After nine years of working there, my legacy at Capital One consisted of lost friendships and mentors. All my doing. I had just reconnected with my former boss, Nigel, after not talking to him for almost a decade. I was grateful he took my call and was open to rebuilding our relationship—and that I was able to apologize for what had happened.

"I don't want to do that again," I said. "But what am I supposed to do? Just pretend these things didn't happen?"

"Instead of vilifying the board, you could go see them and put your perceptions and concerns squarely on the table."

The idea of telling the board my fears seemed crazy, and yet I was determined not to create a destructive departure at Encore. I needed to clear the air.

Shayne helped me prepare for the conversation by outlining my fears and goals. I wanted both to state my perceptions without being accusatory and to remain open to their perspective. We isolated my greatest fear—being rejected—and then turned it on its head. If I was able to accept any outcome, including being told I wasn't the right person for the job, then I could avoid being defensive. After a follow-up discussion, I was ready.

I arranged a meeting with several key board members in the Century City office of one of them, just west of downtown Los Angeles. Driving up, I wondered, *who sets up a meeting to facilitate their own execution?* I kept driving anyway.

I started our discussion by telling them I had struggled with several board decisions. I laid them out and then explained how I had interpreted them. Shayne had drilled me on clearly distinguishing between the facts I had collected and my conclusions about them. Any deviation and I knew I would come across as accusatory and belligerent.

After some hesitation, I asked point-blank the question most troubling me: Were they planning to replace me as the CEO? If so, I assured them I would handle it professionally and do what was best for the company. I paused, both scared and ready to hear whatever they had to say.

They thanked me for coming and putting the topic on the table. "We didn't make these decisions because we want somebody else as CEO. You are the person we want running Encore. But there's a lot going on right now, and we want to be more involved. As a board, we've collectively experienced a great deal and have different perspectives. We need you to explore all possibilities, not just advocate for what you believe is right.

While you're correct on many fronts, you have blind spots and need to learn to rely on others." We spent an hour going through the details of their feedback. I thanked them and left the office.

On the way out of the elevator, I called Dana, who had been giving herself an ulcer, to tell her I still had a job. We talked for most of my drive back to San Diego. For the first time in weeks, I was able to focus on something other than my job status. And I was excited to get back to work.

SHAYNE

Our egosystem and brain can convince us of anything, regardless of its veracity. We can make—I myself have done it countless times—any number of important decisions with profound conviction, only to realize later it wasn't really what we wanted or was based on incorrect perceptions.

Brandon was on the verge of such a decision when we spoke in early 2009. The only telltale sign that his ego was on full alert was his emotional state. He was feeling at the mercy. Instead of following his gut, however, Brandon sought to be curious about his anger, and ultimately he was able to link it back to his ego threats.

Equally important in Brandon's shift was his ability to connect tangibly to the costs he would create if he persisted in his reaction. Having understood the role his egosystem played in his departure from Capital One was instrumental. Brandon's understanding of that conflict had evolved from "they did this to me" to "I was threatened by the changes, lashed out to protect myself, and ultimately damaged important relationships." This is different than flipping from "it's their fault" to "it's my fault." Assigning blame to our self is just as much an egosystem reaction as is blaming others. We are still not in a learning space—although the guilt, in a strange way, makes us feel better because beating ourselves up gives us the ego benefit of proclaiming that we know better without actually changing anything. Instead, Brandon recognized his responsibility for his response to Encore's board members through empathizing with his previous frailties.

Identifying how we contributed to past failures in life means the difference between developing wisdom and repeating the same patterns over and over again. Had Brandon not come to terms with his true motivations in leaving Capital One, he could have blindly repeated them at Encore. In fact, he had already started. Seeing that the last time he fell into this pattern it damaged his legacy and severed relationships for a decade provided Brandon with a dose of emotional clarity. *It allowed him to be guided by what he truly wanted, not by what his egosystem feared.* Although he was anxious, Brandon was irrevocably committed to creating a constructive conversation with the board. At a profound level he preferred hearing that he wasn't capable of being CEO, and leaving Encore productively, than proving it wasn't his fault and leaving destructively.

This shift happened *before* he knew the outcome. He couldn't control what the board members said or did. They might have told him he wasn't the guy. He could only choose what essentials guided him and what quality of relationship he was committed to creating. He "let go of the outcome" while staying firmly committed to his goal.

This wasn't an easy conversation to create. Brandon could have sugarcoated how he truly felt about the situation and, as a result, not really obtained resolution. Or presented his conclusions and frustrations as facts, causing an escalation. Or fished for reassurance that he was the right guy, likely prompting a less than honest response from the board. Being constructive, but also relentless, is a delicate balance. We have identified five crucial aspects of such constructive communication: being vulnerable, empathetic, direct, exploratory, and caring (VEDEC).

CONSTRUCTIVE COMMUNICATION
Vulnerable, Empathetic, Direct, Exploratory, Caring (VEDEC) contrasted with our ego's default self-protective strategies.

Reactive	Authentic (VEDEC)
Protect Myself	Vulnerable
Critical or Harsh	Empathetic
Avoiding (being vague or sugarcoating)	Direct (and Specific)
Being Right (I Know)	Exploratory (or Curious)
Indifferent or Reserved	Caring

1. **Vulnerable.** Whenever we are guarded—acting to cover our natural, human vulnerability—we behave in ways that trigger other people's egosystems. By sharing our ego threats as our own discomfort, we pacify others and give them elements to help them understand us. When we put our core fears out in the open, we no longer have anything to protect; this allows others to empathize with how we are feeling.

   PRACTICE Share your fears about yourself and your intentions for the conversation.

2. **Empathetic.** When we walk in another person's shoes, understanding how we could feel and behave as that person does, it helps us see beyond the other person's behaviors. It also makes us aware of how we would feel if we were on the receiving end of our own reactions and judgments.

   PRACTICE Help the other person name his/her feelings/experience.

3. **Direct.** Being direct is a delicate aspect of constructive communication. Being direct is *not* expressing our judgments in an abrasive fashion. That is unloading our emotional tension with the intent of overpowering the other person and usually shuts others down without actually providing useful content. On the other hand, many leaders sugarcoat their message or make general statements, hoping the other person will get the message. This often leads to the conclusion that the person doesn't want to listen, when in fact the message wasn't really delivered. Being direct is stating our observations in specific language, without agitation or judgment.

   PRACTICE Ask the other person to summarize what he or she heard to see how clear, direct, and specific you have been in delivering your message.

4. **Exploratory.** A key antidote for our addiction to being right is showing a willingness to explore ideas. Instead of advocating for or defending your own point of view, be curious; find out what information you might be missing. What do others think and perceive? What is their context? What do they see that you don't?

   PRACTICE A Clarify what the other person really means.
   PRACTICE B Challenge and expand your own perception.

5. **Caring.** Caring is the intention to support another person's well-being and development. When someone feels vulnerable or threatened, it matters whether we are harsh or indifferent—or invested in our relationship with him or her. As with vulnerability, it helps to create a safe space for both parties.

   PRACTICE Clarify why you care about providing feedback to the other person. What's at stake for him or her?

The challenge is to practice these five skills in unison. Having an exploratory mindset without directness leaves the conversation with no spine. Directness without care or empathy leaves us cold, making the message harder to hear. When we are able to integrate these different aspects of ourselves, even the most delicate conversations become possible.

CHAPTER 6

YOUR EGO LOVES AN ENEMY

The Destructive Effects of the "Offensive" Ego

BRANDON

"What should we bid?" asked Amy a few weeks later in an Investment Committee meeting in February 2009.

For the past three years, the answer to that question had been simple: "It doesn't matter because we won't win anyway." But now everything was different.

"The question is how low should we bid," said Paul. "The last thing we want to do is overpay."

Paul's response summed up how we all felt. The financial collapse after September 2008 had decimated our industry. We believed that only one or two competitors were able to bid on this opportunity; a year earlier, that number had been closer to twenty. At Encore we had stayed disciplined for a long time and now it was finally going to pay off. The time we spent creating a new, positive dynamic in the IC was producing immediate returns. Our conversations were both blunt and exploratory, and we felt supremely confident our decisions would take full advantage of the upcoming opportunities.

If only our shareholders felt as confident. They were still convinced Encore was going down in flames. Most believed that the economic collapse was impacting our customers more than other financial institutions, and they were forecasting a dramatic drop in our revenues. Paul and I were constantly fielding questions and assuring our shareholders that we had planned for just this window of opportunity. Despite that, our stock price continued to free-fall. While the economic crisis brought the overall market down 35 percent, Encore's stock was trading below $4. It had lost 80 percent of its value in six months. I may have solidified my status with the board, but it didn't make me feel secure. I'm a huge sports fan and know that when teams lose, the manager gets fired.

Despite the market's lack of faith, my executive team was firing on all cylinders. Nobody panicked or quit. Historical enemies, our Finance and Operations teams finalized an activity cost database that tracked every operating activity and assigned the cost to each individual account. This allowed our Decision Science team to build incredibly precise profitability models. Instead of fighting over who was right, departments were using each other's expertise to raise our game to a new level.

Most significant, total collections in India were up 200 percent. The pilot team formed in 2008 to manage higher-quality consumer accounts continued performing on par with the domestic call centers. It was no fluke. Given that, our HR team was diligently working on hiring plans for both India and the United States, and there were no lingering discussions about the merits of expanding our presence in India. Several domestic call center leaders volunteered to spend months in India helping out. We were starting to shine.

We discussed these results at our April board meeting and everybody was encouraged. As usual, the board held an executive session without the management team to discuss any concerns or questions.

Toward the end of that session, one of the board members called me in, which was not common. He said the board was excited about what was happening and wanted to take full advantage of the opportunities ahead. They wanted me to concentrate on running the business day-to-day and had asked Encore's chairman, George Lund, to support me by managing some of the administrative functions and helping drive the corporate strategy. They felt the combination of our strengths would be powerful, and that Encore would be better equipped to succeed.

I stared blankly at him. *What?!*

The board had decided to make George Encore's executive chairman. In this new role, he would spend a significant amount of time in our offices. Paul and Sharon, along with our general counsel, would report directly to him, with a dotted line to me. I would focus primarily on Operations, Technology, and Business Development.

In most companies, my "new" role was called chief operating officer, not chief executive officer.

Holy shit. I was right all along. They were planning something. I just got the signals wrong. They didn't want to fire me; they wanted me to become the COO again.

Different friends had told me it was common for new investors to bring in their "guy." That was George. I was crushed. The emotional roller coaster was going to kill me.

I went home and told Dana about the decision.

"You got demoted?" she asked.

"The technical answer is no, but it sure seems that way."

"How do you feel?"

Everything from indignant to fatalistic. I couldn't believe this change was being made now, when the hard work of the last few years was finally paying dividends.

"What are you going to tell the team?" she asked.

"I haven't even thought about it." They would all have the same questions. I often counseled people not to "go into the wreckage of the future" because the scenarios they imagined rarely materialized. It was a waste of time to sit around and be a conspiracy theorist. Despite that, I spent the entire night coming up with thousands of nightmare scenarios and embarrassing questions that would come my way once the news became public. I couldn't imagine a single positive outcome from this change.

By morning, I was sure everyone at the company would judge me a failure, and the shareholders would lose respect for me. They certainly had the facts to support their case. My Encore tombstone would read: "Here lies Brandon Black, former CEO. He took over Encore with the stock at $20 per share and brought it down to $3. Good riddance." A part of me recognized that my ego was triggered, but it was too painful to face.

I had no time to process anything, however, because George and I were scheduled to tell the executive team about the change that day, April 29, 2009. I needed to put on a good show and be supportive. Encore was paying my bills, and I was resolved not to be destructive. That didn't make me feel better, but it did allow me to get into the car and drive to work.

"I want to be very clear about this," George said to my team. "There is only one CEO at Encore and that is Brandon. I have a day job and am only here to help. It is my sincerest hope that one plus one will equal three. We're going to have a lot of fun."

What else could he say? He couldn't tell people the truth, that the board was demoting me. At least my business cards still said CEO; that would make it easier to find a new job.

I looked around the room to gauge people's reactions. They looked back at me, doing the same. I just smiled and nodded along with George's points. When he was done, I told everybody how excited I was to have George help us achieve our goals. I'm not sure how well I sold it.

There would be a press release later that day announcing the management change along with our first quarter's earnings. I had to keep up the charade for the entire day. The painful irony was that this was the moment we proved all our doubters wrong. Our first quarter's results were significantly higher than predicted. Cash collections were up 10 percent and earnings by 30 percent. We were deploying capital for new purchases at an increasing rate. I knew the stock market would respond favorably, and it did. By the end of the week, our stock price was above $12 per share, a 400 percent increase since the low point in February, just 60 days before. I should have been shouting from the rooftop.

George and I met in my office after the meeting. "I thought everything went great," said George.

"Couldn't agree more," I responded. *Are you kidding me? You swoop in just as we're taking off. Where were you when we couldn't buy anything and India was flailing? You get to walk around the office today and have a great time with the employees celebrating our success. I, on the other hand, get to explain how exciting it is to be marginalized.*

I held all my mind chatter in as we exchanged pleasantries. I couldn't get away fast enough. As we emerged, I saw Jim Syran waiting outside my office. He wanted to grab a few seconds of my time, and I obliged. When I closed the door, he blurted out, "Dude, they just demoted you. What's up with that?" I didn't know what to say. This was exactly what I feared would happen.

I spent the next few weeks fearful of additional changes to come while simultaneously generating lists in my mind of all George's shortcomings. When nothing happened for a month, I decided to make the best of a bad situation. I wasn't going to quit, and I assumed all the work I had done with LaL would allow me to stop reacting to George. But it didn't. Why should he get any credit for the work I did? I knew it wasn't productive, but I couldn't help it—it was all true. Over the next few months, I added more flaws. I couldn't believe how much time he spent on trivial items.

"Why don't we change the board package?" George asked me one day.

"We've had the same package for a decade," I responded. "It seems to work fine."

"I don't like how it flows, and we don't have the right emphasis in the beginning. Also, I think you should talk less."

What the hell is he talking about? We're paying you all this money, and you're worried about how the board package flows and how much I speak? Shouldn't you be thinking about how to expand the company or something? On top of it all, when we were challenged about the new format in the next board meeting, I looked toward him to answer. He didn't say a word. Par for the course.

Board package layouts, press release language, getting new offices, feedback about how to be more sensitive to board members' perspectives. This wasn't elementary school. Where were the strategic revelations?

It was glaringly clear how much better I was than him. How could the board have put him above me? But he was my boss and could fire me if he wanted. I promised Dana I would not do anything stupid. *Just suck it up and play along.*

That didn't mean I couldn't talk about the situation outside the office. Friends, family, and anyone not affiliated with Encore got an earful. The group that heard about it the most was my Young Presidents' Organization (YPO) Forum. Each of these individuals ran companies, so I knew they would understand the injustice. The beauty in all these discussions was that I had the ability to pick and choose what facts I felt were relevant. And because there was no way for anybody to have enough context to question my assessment, I was able to build my own personal support group. I was a great martyr.

When I had time alone, however, I found myself feeling unsettled and wondering if there was more to this than I was willing to acknowledge. Intellectually, I knew I was at the mercy of George and the situation. I thought that would have been enough to push me to act differently, to not fall back into my counterproductive behaviors. But I was doing exactly the opposite. It was almost like I couldn't help myself.

SHAYNE

The seemingly unjust and unjustified appointment of George Lund to executive chairman in 2009 infected Brandon's work experience. He was sure he was being displaced, and nothing George said to the contrary could convince him otherwise. Meanwhile, Encore's performance continued to improve, justifying Brandon's resistance to the new setup. However aware Brandon was of his triggers, he was unable to exit his prolonged state of pinch. In coaching calls, Brandon overwhelmed my attempts at finding a different perspective with stories of George's latest outrageous transgressions. This was Brandon's *reality*.

Brandon identified the ego threats of being trivialized, no longer respected, and judged a failure. Like most of the examples we've explored in previous chapters, these self-worth anxieties stemmed from the part of his egosystem that wanted to protect him from harm, humiliation, and discomfort—his *"defensive ego."* But George's role also threatened Brandon's self-image of success. Remember, he grew up with the drive to be #1. He thrived on having the right answer, being the smartest person in the room, and seeking the high of feeling admired, even revered. This was his "*offensive ego*." Brandon was being triggered from both sides.

Our egosystem isn't governed just by fear. As people and leaders, we want acknowledgment, recognition, and success. We yearn to be the go-to person, the ultimate visionary offering the missing insight. We want others to need us, to look up to us, to accept us. When we know the answer or deliver the impossible, we feel worthy, powerful, superior. We glow with assurance, and reassurance, that we really are as amazing as we dreamed. This is our offensive ego in action—striving not to avoid judgment but to gain status.

Although uncomfortable, it is nonetheless easier to focus on the fear-based emotions of our defensive ego, because they're more recognizable and in line with our values. We're the ones being hurt or judged, so we're in the "good" role. As the victim, we feel justified lashing out. The offensive ego, on the other hand, isn't humble or generous. It knows it's right. It greedily wants to be the smartest, the strongest, the most competent. To shine over others. If you recognize this in yourself, you're in good company; it's a common tendency at all levels of leadership. If your mind is insisting, "I'm not like that!" well, that's your ego talking.

This aggressive desire to prove ourselves comes in many forms. It keeps us late at the office, drives feelings of comparison with others, and can trigger our most destructive interpersonal behaviors. As Steve Macadam, the CEO of a global diversified manufacturing company, once remarked, "I always prided myself on mentoring and growing my team. And then I discovered that my need to be the smartest person in the room was preventing me from letting anyone have a better idea than me. I was actually holding people back despite my professed desire to unleash their full potential."

Another frequently seen offensive ego leadership dysfunction is the hero syndrome, where a leader thrives on saving the day: resurrecting a project in crisis, or turning around a failing organization. I understand. The feeling of being indispensable and uber-competent while others struggle is candy-heroin for our egosystem. Plus, our environments often reinforce these behaviors by giving more recognition for solving a crisis than for preventing one. We glorify tales of individuals making a superhuman effort, not of teams methodically building the foundation for tomorrow's success. Not coincidentally, the "hero" leader often shoots from the hip, rarely finding time to mentor people or build processes. The frantic activity of this reactive leadership dysfunction creates the crises we'll have to fix tomorrow. We're *pyromaniac firemen.*

By the time George was made executive chairman, Brandon had been working for some time to let go of his offensive ego desires. "After several years of poor executive hires," Brandon explained, "I realized that my need to be admired prevented me from actually hiring people who were better or more competent than me."

But letting go of an ego driver is different from having it blown up by surprise against our will. George's appointment threatened Brandon's semiconscious craving to be revered. Since the ego sees the world through a zero-sum lens, his relentless judgment of George aimed to preserve Brandon's primacy.

This is among the greatest costs of our offensive ego: Our insatiable need for acknowledgment causes us to knock others down. We exert power over people and groups not because we are evil, but because our ego believes we'll be adored or untouchable if we're on top. Our egosystem has mistaken admiration for love, without realizing it won't ever satisfy us.

Luckily, there's a way out of this prison.

Taking Back Our Creative Power

BRANDON

During a coaching call in August 2009, I was updating Shayne on how things were going: Everything was great except for George. He had missed a call earlier that day, which reinforced my beliefs about his lack of commitment. I was tired of being jerked around by his unpredictable schedule. We had some important decisions to make, and I didn't want to keep pushing them back. But he was my boss and I couldn't force him to do anything.

"How would you interact with George if the roles were reversed?" asked Shayne. "What if he worked for you?"

"Are we playing a hypothetical game?" I responded. "That's ridiculous."

"Your frustrations are making you give up your power and sense of direction, but you're the one here for the long term. You are the CEO, and Encore is your company. If George worked for you, you'd want to get the most out of him, wouldn't you?"

"I would."

"So if George worked for you, what skills would you leverage from him?"

I hadn't spent much time thinking about his strengths, so I said what came to mind.

"Well, he is an excellent relationship builder, especially when it comes to the board. He is a good negotiator. In fact, without him we wouldn't have resolved a massive dispute we had with another company. He reads people well and seems to know what questions to ask around strategic opportunities."

"So, he does have positive qualities that are valuable to Encore. Given how quickly you came up with those, there are probably others you would identify if you approached the relationship differently."

Shayne paused. "What has George done to suggest he is trying to take over your job?"

"Besides the long list I already gave you?" I responded sarcastically. I did *not* want to see George in a positive light. "Have you been paying attention at all?"

He laughed. "I haven't yet heard a fact that supports your fear that George wants to be CEO. Most of the time, you're complaining he's too hands-off. So which is it?

"I think this is more about you having to be the best CEO," Shayne continued. "Think about how you engage the difficult personalities on your team. You've really learned to see past their flaws and draw out their strengths—except with George. That can't be a coincidence. Maybe he does some things better than you? If you're serious about making the most of his strengths for Encore's benefit, take a learning intention in your next few meetings with him. What could it hurt?"

"It'll be a waste of time," I said as we hung up.

I spent the next few days trying to prove Shayne wrong, but there wasn't any evidence. Neither the board nor George had done anything to undermine my credibility. The data didn't support my hypothesis. There had to be another reason for my attitude and actions. Until I understood it, I knew I wouldn't be able to shift my behavior. But I was tired of looking in the mirror; I just couldn't seem to summon up the effort.

I was walking the floor the next day, saying hello to different account managers, when I remembered a promise I had made during the layoffs back in 2007. With 1,000 employees and their families counting on me, I had committed to make the right decision for Encore, no matter how uncomfortable it was for my ego. Since then, that number had almost doubled. *It is not acceptable to let my ego run the show.* Remembering that decision gave me the fortitude to interrogate my fears.

I talked my difficulty over with Dana and then with Paul, who had become a close friend I trusted without reservation. Instead of griping about George, I focused our conversations on my behaviors. He remembered something I told him after returning from a seminar; that my unconscious, ego-fueled goal was to be publicly recognized as a great leader. Maybe George's presence threatened that?

Something rang true in his inquiry. I knew my ego competed to be #1, and George's new role moved me squarely into the #2 position. But his insertion into Encore threatened something even more important: my ability to view myself as a success. I had built an amazing team that was doing incredible things. We were on the cusp of producing fabulous results. Finally, people would notice and see me as a great leader, not a quitter. Deep down, I really wanted to get the credit for Encore's success, and George's presence was robbing me of that. I had been making him pay, but in doing so I was undermining him and his potential contribution, putting Encore's goals and employees at risk.

It was a powerful moment of clarity. I actually felt different. My head felt lighter, and my pent-up aggravation with George ebbed. Without knowing it, I had become the star in my own reality television series. These months of drama were self-inflicted. I resolved to learn from George and not compete with him. To do so, I needed a mantra. *He isn't here to take my job. He's doing whatever he can to help Encore move forward.*

For the next few months, I had good days with George and bad days. The good days occurred when I took the time to consider other possibilities for his actions. When he needed to reschedule something, I reminded myself that he had significant responsibilities as the CEO of another company. It wasn't automatically a lack of commitment to Encore. As new strategic opportunities emerged, I began to seek George out for guidance on how to approach them, including asking him to participate from the beginning. He had handled many acquisitions throughout his career, while Encore had done only one. The more I was proactive and open to his input, the more quickly my judgments subsided, and the more invaluable his experience became.

I came to appreciate George's counsel and wisdom. He helped me think more strategically and to be patient with the board. He always seemed to take a long-term approach and didn't get rattled by short-term fluctuations. The one thing I could never figure out is why he bothered with simple things like the board package. One day I finally asked.

"It's not that the old format didn't work," he explained. "But I wanted to give visibility to the broader leadership team. The new format and my request that you speak less were designed to give the board more comfort around your leadership, not less."

"Not following," I responded.

"Since I joined the board in 2007, you were the only one who answered when questions arose. That gave the board two fundamental questions: Is he the only one with any answers? And how can somebody know everything? By giving more of a voice to your team, we addressed both concerns."

We talked more about how I could better understand Encore's place in the overall perspective of my board members. Too often, I came at issues solely from my perspective without taking into account what they were balancing.

"You've got to remember that they all have day jobs and other investments that demand their attention. They can only spend a fraction of their time on Encore. You, on the other hand, have one priority. The more time you spend understanding their other priorities and any associated challenges, the more you can be an effective partner."

As usual, his feedback was clear, well reasoned, and spot-on. He was never trying to "steal the spotlight" from me. In fact, he consistently went out of his way to help me improve the areas where I needed to grow. He challenged me to be more visible outside of Encore and to make sure we were well-known within the communities where we did business.

I had initially hated the board's decision to appoint George as executive chairman. I had silently resisted and focused on how useless he was. But without me saying anything to him, and without him changing, I discovered that he was a key resource I needed to listen to in order to grow and succeed as CEO.

SHAYNE

Without realizing it, George went through a metamorphosis during his first months as Encore's executive chairman: from useless deadweight to key strategic partner. What happened?

The critical attitude Brandon held toward George was similar to other struggling relationships at Encore: the self-fulfilling prophecies that Brandon had with Dave, Fritz, and the directors; the Finance vs. Operations Us vs. Them; the undermining of the India strategy. In each case, people experienced their frustration as true, when in fact they were unconsciously focusing on the negative in others. Worse, when we do this, our mindset and behaviors actually influence others to be less than their best selves, either because they don't feel safe or because we simply don't allow them to participate. We limit their potential. At LaL we call this "making others bad."

Most of the dysfunctions outlined in this book, including those mentioned above, are examples of making bad. Whenever we are in our reactive state or at the mercy, our protective behaviors have negative, undermining consequences on others. We feel like victims but are simultaneously the victimizers. Brandon felt hurt and undermined by George's presence at Encore, and yet his behaviors sought to undermine and exclude George. Brandon wanted Encore to succeed, and yet he was acting to minimize George's usefulness. No one, including Brandon, gets up in the morning and goes to the office planning to make his or her colleagues bad. But we do it all the time. Even being intellectually aware of our ego triggers is sometimes insufficient, as Brandon's struggle with George illustrates.

The point is not whether George had flaws, but rather *where Brandon was putting his mental focus.* When we recognize we're in a making bad mindset, we open the door to a different path forward.

At the heart of transforming ourselves, our organizations, and our lives is the empowering decision to *"make others good."* It is an indispensable step in shifting from at the mercy to at the source.

Making good is not becoming responsible for changing other people, nor guaranteeing their success.

Nor is it making people feel good, being nice, or sucking it up and never complaining. It is not holding in our frustrations and criticisms until we burst.

It is not relinquishing our point of view and sweeping our disagreements under the rug.

And no, making good is definitely not blindly trusting that others will do the right thing.

At its essence, making good is taking back our creative power.

It starts with a "never again" decision: a refusal to blindly continue *our own* egosystem behaviors. Our never again is rooted in our awareness of how our ego triggers cause us to act out, to shut down in destructive ways, or to devalue others. We saw this moment with Brandon, when he recalled his commitment to never again allow his ego to negatively affect the employees and families of Encore. He didn't know what was really going on for him, nor had he yet changed his opinion of George. He started by not accepting being destructive toward others in order to protect his ego.

Just as making bad is a mental orientation, making good is also a mindset—*to be the starting point of your experience and growth, regardless of outside circumstances.* If you examine your life you will notice that whenever you feel at the mercy, you are making others—and likely yourself—bad. When we make good, we take back our power. We take ownership for how we internalize people and external circumstances. In doing so, we stop perpetuating an egosystem-driven culture.

We have seen many examples of making good in Brandon's and Encore's story. When Jim walked the floor at the Phoenix call center, being emotionally present for people's pain and acknowledging them as equally vulnerable human beings. When Brandon responded to Jonathan's angry questions about India in the town hall meeting by searching with empathy to understand what people in the room were feeling. He acknowledged their fears as legitimate while not letting go of his intention for them and the organization, nor changing the India strategy. When Brandon and his team violated conventional wisdom to give high-quality accounts to Encore's Indian collectors, they broke through the invisible ways they were undermining their colleagues' full potential.

Sometimes making others good requires having an explicit, uncomfortable conversation, like when Brandon had a conversation with Dave or with the board members, implementing the five aspects of constructive communication LaL refers to as VEDEC: being vulnerable, empathetic, direct, exploratory, and caring. On the other hand, sometimes no overt conversation is needed. Brandon didn't raise his frustrations with George. He simply began viewing and interacting with George with a different intent. He accepted the vulnerable feelings of perceiving himself as less than George, which allowed him to appreciate and learn from him.

In relationships or situations that are very difficult, making good may seem impossible. I get it.

A decade ago, my firm engaged a consultant to work with our own team. The first year was very helpful, but the relationship blew up in year two. The atmosphere in our company became quite negative, and the consultant and another employee quit and pursued our largest client.

I found myself trying to pick up the pieces. I had every reason to judge this person. I even had a trump card that justified limitless righteousness: Her attempt to steal a client from us was absolutely *unethical*.

Trust me, I blamed, I churned in the middle of the night, I vented. All of that made me feel like the good guy—*and* completely at the mercy. How in the world could I make *that* good?

Making her good wasn't accepting that she was right or faultless, nor was it condoning her actions. But in seeking to make that whole experience good *for me*, opportunities presented themselves. First, it reconnected me with the many ways in which she was initially immensely helpful. Changes that still exist today and that I don't want to lose. Making good also pushed me to confront how I helped bring about the crisis in the first place—ways in which I wasn't taking responsibility for the leadership of the firm. And being on the receiving end of a destructive consultant taught me to be more vigilant about how I work with my own clients.

None of this was accessible to me as long as I was in a making bad mindset. Who really pays the price when we fill our brains with blame instead of learning? If Brandon had continued to make George bad, it was his own growth that would have been damaged.

Making good also forces us to take a hard look at our view of reality. The perception gap between Brandon and George during those first months was fascinating—and points to the power of our egosystem to deform our perception.

"I was very careful to only interact with the Encore team through the Executive Committee that Brandon, Paul, and I formed," George explained later. "I didn't want to undermine Brandon's authority in any way. More than anything, the change in my role was aimed at making me the point person for the board, not a co-executive of Encore."

While Brandon felt threatened by the board's apparent decision to carve up his role, George had neither mandate nor interest in supplanting him. What Brandon criticized as George's lack of commitment—not actively managing Encore's business functions—George consciously chose not to take on in order to support Brandon's authority as CEO. "I know that intent was said clearly," George recalled, "but Brandon just couldn't hear it."

This highlights another danger of making bad—when our mental faculties are devoured by ego fears and fault finding, it disrupts our fundamental ability to assimilate contradictory information. Brandon's lack of understanding had nothing to do with his obvious intelligence. I have seen this phenomena dozens of times over the years in very senior executives. He simply *could not integrate* that George's intentions were different from what he feared. Not I, not Brandon's YPO members, nor other colleagues or friends were able to make more than a small dent in Brandon's conclusions.

The question I asked Brandon, "If he worked for you, what skills would you want to leverage?" wasn't a rhetorical trick. I was searching for a perspective that would bring Brandon back to a mindset where he was *the starting point of what he wanted to create* at Encore. As long as Brandon was at the mercy of his perceptions, George would remain an albatross rather than an invaluable contributor.

I find it fascinating that Brandon's shift did not come from challenging his assumptions. Instead, *shifting his orientation from making bad to making good allowed his mind to discern a more accurate perspective*. Reconnecting with what he wanted to create, regardless of external circumstances, allowed him to see and use George in a completely different way. Brandon had found his inner compass again.

Being willing to learn from George also meant accepting to not be #1, sharing the spotlight, and acknowledging weaknesses he still had as a CEO. Over the next few years, his breadth of effectiveness expanded as he learned skills from George that weren't accessible to him as long as he was in unconscious competition with him. "I didn't know what I was missing," Brandon later said, "and I wasn't able to see what George had to teach me until I began making him good."

CHAPTER 7

WE CAN'T TALK ABOUT "THAT" (MEET AMY ANUK)

———

BRANDON

A key leadership change during 2009 was the promotion of Amy Anuk to vice president of Business Development. Over six years, Amy evolved from an entry-level analyst to one of the most important executives in the company. Her team was charged with identifying and negotiating all portfolio purchases. If they were ineffective, Encore was unsuccessful. The board of directors unanimously approved her promotion, and she had the firm support of the management team. I knew she was up to the job. The sky was the limit for her.

Amy's story is a great example of what was possible at Encore. We prided ourselves on hiring and promoting people based exclusively on their capabilities, not their resume, years of experience, or other such factors. We had a true meritocracy, with no biases.

Or so I thought.

In the years since her promotion, I learned that she didn't perceive her rise to the top as quick or anything like the smooth trajectory I saw. It made me question whether all Encore's employees were truly given an equal chance to succeed. The answer isn't straightforward, and her story taught me a lot.

Our Egosystem's Biases and Blind Spots

AMY

My name is Amy Anuk. Early in my employment at Encore, one remark changed the course of my career.

It was mid-2003, and my supervisor sat me down to talk about my career options.

"You have three paths you could go down," he said. "Transition into marketing, join IT as a business analyst, or pursue a career in business development."

Three choices?! I was thrilled. I had only joined Encore for a specific media project. Now, I had someone helping me explore my options.

"Given your skill set, I think the best bet is business development. When I was talking it over with the CEO, however, he was concerned that a woman couldn't be effective in this role. Still, I think you have real potential."

I kept smiling as the conversation continued, but inside I was fuming. *Can't be effective? How dare the CEO tell me I can't do this?!* Whatever questions I had about what I *wanted* to do with my career evaporated as one thought burned through me: *prove him, them, wrong.*

I threw myself into learning the ropes of business development with single-minded determination. The role entailed being responsible for securing and developing sales relationships as well as creating, negotiating, and leading portfolio purchase transactions. It was an externally facing role in an industry where newcomers had to earn respect from "industry veterans" before they were taken seriously. The key decision makers at the banks were predominantly men who had been doing business with the same people for a very long time.

Despite my overwhelming determination to succeed, I had doubts in the back of my mind about whether I could build enough rapport with people in this tight network. Immediately I began identifying senior leaders at Encore who had influence, and I studied people across the industry I needed to establish a strong relationship with. Since I didn't fit the expected demographic, I concluded that I needed to get their attention by delivering results and outperforming everyone else. *I needed to shine.*

I set three objectives: (1) always exceed expectations; (2) don't let anyone see my flaws or weaknesses; and (3) keep my personal life separate from my professional life—all business, all the time.

Over the next several years, I outperformed and received promotions. Then, in 2005, my manager and a colleague resigned from the company within the same week. I was the only person left from a three-person team.

Brandon, by now the CEO, called me into his office. "Amy," he said, looking at me, "we need you."

His words were all I needed to hear. It was my time to prove I was ready and capable of leading the department. For the next year, reporting to Dave, our head of Operations, I acted as Encore's Business Development leader and performed well, delivering on expectations.

One day, out of the blue, Dave pulled me aside.

"You're doing a great job, Amy," he said, "but we need someone with more experience. We've begun recruiting for your new boss. I didn't want you to find out through the grapevine. You'll be on the interview panel, of course," he added as he walked away.

The decision blindsided me. I didn't understand. I hadn't failed. I was getting plenty of praise and recognition. *I delivered everything asked of me.*

No one sat down with me to discuss why I wasn't getting the job, and I didn't hear a justifiable, logical reason for being passed over. Dave's transactional exchange with me felt callous and insensitive. Not wanting to appear weak or give them anything to hold against me, I bottled up what I felt and vowed to be even more capable—to be so perfectly outstanding that they could not deny me.

I eventually bought into the idea of working for someone from whom I could learn. As we went through the interview process, one candidate with comparable skills to mine seemed a good fit for our team, but not as the leader. Dave and I agreed to offer him a job at my level, senior manager. Several weeks later, however, I returned to my desk to find an envelope sitting on my chair. I opened it and discovered the offer letter to him from Encore—for a more senior, director-level position making significantly more money. HR must have left it for me because I was the highest-ranking (and only) person on the Business Development team. I stormed into Dave's office seeking an explanation.

"Amy, people get paid different amounts for different reasons," Dave explained. "In this case, we had to pay the market rate to get the person to accept. In addition, he was already at the director level, so we needed to keep his title consistent. It isn't personal. Why are you so agitated?"

Market rate? If that was what people should be paid, why was my salary so low? Didn't I deserve to be paid "at the market"? Not wanting to be labeled as high maintenance, I decided to let it go. I was promoted to director shortly thereafter.

A few months later, we finally hired a new SVP. Although I supported the choice at the time, it quickly became evident there wasn't a big gap between his capabilities and mine. I didn't see what I was going to learn from him. Not wanting to undermine the hiring decision, though, I kept quiet. The longer he stayed in the job, however, the clearer the underlying message seemed to be. Even though I was capable, I didn't "fit" the mold of who they were looking for in a senior leader. I was ready to leave Encore.

With nothing to lose, I approached Brandon and asked him for a substantial pay increase and the ability to commute from Los Angeles. My husband's job was based in LA and required a lot of travel. We didn't see each other very much, and moving to LA would allow us to be more connected. I expected Brandon to say "no" or negotiate heavily with me. But, without hesitating, he agreed to my requests. I still believed I deserved a higher position, but the changes gave me enough incentive to stay. I would prove to him that I could succeed as an executive.

SHAYNE

Let's say it straight up: Amy felt that she was passed over and underpaid because she was a woman.

Was this true?

Was it intentional?

If it were *un*intentional, would or should it make a difference to how she felt?

Or were there factors she wasn't taking into account that explained why certain decisions were made?

How could Amy have tested her assumptions without other people perceiving that she was accusing them of discrimination?

Individual and institutional sexism and racism exist in both blatant and subtle forms. Most of us, despite being well meaning, carry implicit biases that affect our experiences and decisions. Unfortunately, we typically have no idea we have them. It took Brandon and his team multiple conversations and a "why not?" experiment to realize that their Indian collectors could be as effective as their American counterparts. They had no ill intent, and as soon as they realized that their beliefs were inaccurate, they cast them aside. Although we all have assumptions to interrogate, the bar of self-awareness is higher for leaders and executives. Undetected prejudices, especially in people in powerful positions, have far-reaching emotional and material consequences.

Often, however, these situations are more complex than we realize. Amy had encountered a series of challenging professional experiences, each one plausibly, but not necessarily, linked to her gender. As we'll discover, Brandon and other male leaders at Encore were slow to see her struggles or recognize their own possible biases. At the same time, Amy's perceptions also may have been biased, and her behaviors may have contributed to the situation. Although tempting, we resist the impulse to analyze whether or not Amy was the victim of sexism. Such a conclusion would be speculative at best, with victims and perpetrators. Instead, we'll focus on how understanding our egosystem can empower us to take effective action.

Let's start with Amy. Over the course of her career, different experiences had led her to conclude that conversations about being passed over were dangerous. "I didn't want to know the truth if they thought I wasn't qualified," Amy recalled. Research shows that it is tricky for women to raise questions about the role that gender may be playing in their workplace experiences. If they broach the subject, they risk being seen as "overly sensitive" or "shrill"; if they show upset, they can be viewed as "an emotional mess"; if they press the issue, they are deemed "too demanding."

Amy, like each of us, was limited by her egosystem. She censored her feelings and didn't express her frustration because she didn't want to appear weak or needy. These completely understandable fears are dreaded images. She also had desired images of appearing to be a team player and a supportive, constructive, and agreeable coworker. Anyone—man or woman—at the mercy of protecting this set of images will likely avoid expressing disagreement or frustration. As in Fritz's relationship with Brandon, Amy didn't feel sufficiently safe to voice her concerns out loud. Instead, she stayed quiet and channeled her resentment into "proving them wrong."

Predictably, her unexpressed frustration built up until one event was too painful to swallow. When a prospective male colleague was offered a higher position and salary, her avoidance flipped to aggression. This avoid, avoid, avoid, attack mechanism is characteristic of conflict avoiders. We hold in our feelings like a pressure cooker until our top blows and all the steam comes out at once. Simply put, being at the mercy of our egosystem hampers any dialogue or evolution.

Compounding this challenge for many women and minorities is an additional, unsettling doubt: "Is this happening because I'm a woman?" "Would I be treated differently if I were white?"

The difficulties of asking such a question are not limited to Amy's ego threats. Anyone on the *receiving* end of such a communication often experiences a severe sense of threat. I, for example, grew up as a straight, educated, white Anglo-Saxon Protestant, and it never occurred to me that my beliefs or actions might be biased against another person. My childhood was difficult, and I was acutely aware of the familial and economic obstacles I had to overcome. What I didn't notice were hurdles I avoided or privileges I received as a young white man belonging to an extended family that was well educated and largely middle class. If I didn't encounter a hurdle, it didn't exist for me, so it didn't come naturally to see how it might exist for someone else. It's taken me years to realize—and I'm still learning—that women and minorities often face hurdles I do not.

Although I aspire to create a world with level playing fields in organizations, being questioned about any of my biased judgments would prompt reactions of shame and defensiveness. If Amy came into my office, as she did Dave's, demanding an explanation for an unjust title and compensation offer, it would trigger my dreaded images. I'd be afraid of appearing unfair, wrong, and thoughtless. If, in addition, there were even a hint of race- or gender-based accusation, my dreaded images would explode: Neanderthal, sexist, victimizer, oppressor, selfish, and overall terrible person.

Unless I was able to notice these images (through a fireball of pinches), my brain would be incapable of pausing and asking, "Hmm, could I have overlooked something? Did I discount Amy inadvertently by not giving her credit the same way I might a man? What can I and we learn together right now?"

Instead, appearing sexist would mortify me, and I would react to save myself: justify my decisions, minimize her experience, and if I could, blame her for overreacting. Not because I consciously wanted to perpetuate an old boys' network. But, in that moment of pinch, my intention to support equality in the workplace would vanish, submerged by my egosystem's visceral need to avoid being seen as an oppressive white male.

I do not offer these reflections to condone my or any white man's defensiveness—just as noting how Amy was at the mercy of her dreaded images does not make anything her fault. My aim, instead, is to highlight how our egosystem causes misunderstanding, alienation, and stalled progress. *When we are at the mercy of our ego threats, these complex issues become treacherous and terrifying to explore.* So we hold our thoughts in, or blurt them out. We judge, defend our view as right, and essentially remove any possibility of learning—about ourselves, the other, or the situation. Together, we prolong the problem.

When George Lund was put in his executive chairman role, Brandon experienced injustice, humiliation, and anger at what he felt was an unwarranted decision. Imagine if he were a woman or a person of color. It would have been difficult for him not to wonder, "Is this because I'm a (fill in the blank)?" Even without this additional layer, Brandon struggled for months to move beyond his resentment and explore the possibility that he was missing either context or important skills and experience (both of which turned out to be the case).

For Amy, her inability to raise these issues, and her not-unjustified fear that others would not be receptive, prevented her from getting a clearer picture of reality, ironing out any misunderstandings, and/or repairing any wrongdoings. Maybe others' preconceived notions of her needed to be shattered. Maybe Amy had skill gaps that needed to be closed before she was ready to take on the role. Likely both. At this point, Amy and her colleagues didn't collectively have the awareness or tools to step into this uncomfortable exploration.

That was beginning to change.

Our Behavioral Patterns Shape the Course of Our Life

AMY

In 2009, Brandon invited me to lunch—always a sure sign he had a specific topic to discuss. He had fired my boss. "I am promoting you to the vice president role," he said. "Effective today, you report directly to me." He laid out the timing of the changes.

At last! I thought. *I'm the one you should have taken all along.* In my excitement, I didn't even realize that my VP title was still one notch below the *senior* vice president title my two predecessors had held. At least I was finally the leader of the team.

"However," he continued, "I need you to work on your leadership style within the company. You come across as a perfect little put-together package that no one can relate to. You're like a robot. You're not approachable."

It was a shocking assessment. I thought my relationships internally were good. They were completely professional and transactional, but, of course, that was deliberate. I was assertive, driven; I got stuff done. Sure, I sometimes offended others with my direct communication style—but not approachable or relatable? I was just mimicking the behaviors of the men whose level of influence and authority I craved.

LaL's one-year program was recommended as development for Encore's executives, and so I signed up, not really sure what to expect. In preparation for my first seminar, they gathered 360-degree feedback, and I wondered whether Brandon's assessment of me would prove to be just his opinion. Instead, the comments were undeniable. Overwhelmingly, there were themes of being unwelcoming, even intimidating. I set high standards and was judgmental and critical if my team didn't meet them. There were perceptions that I didn't tolerate failure for myself or for anyone working for me. I was described as uncaring, direct, selfish, and aggressive. What hurt the most, however, was that some of my colleagues openly questioned my motives. Apparently, it was widely perceived that I would do whatever it took to get a deal done, whether profitable or not. When I encountered resistance, I ran over anyone who got in the way.

The feedback hurt. The comments from my team and my peers made me revisit the objectives I chose years earlier to prove my competence at all costs. It was the first time I had heard so directly how my desire to be the best and prove my doubters wrong impacted the people around me.

While I was stunned by the unintended consequences, I also was confused about why my approach was creating such a backlash. The same behaviors I had observed and learned from successful men were being seen in me as aggressive, offensive, too results focused, and intimidating. They were undermining, not enhancing, my effectiveness as a leader.

I attended my first leadership seminar and began reflecting on why I had intentionally avoided showing any stereotypical female traits, like care, concern, or emotion. I feared that any "softness" would cause me to be seen as not strong enough—to the extent that in six years at Encore, I had only ever worn pantsuits. I needed to appear powerful enough to earn the respect of men. And the line between my professional and my personal life was impenetrable. I didn't want being a woman to hold me back in this job, at this company, in this industry.

My LaL coach, Carole Levy, nudged me to be more vulnerable and honest with myself. I began to realize that my aversion to appearing weak ran deeper than my job. I grew up in a modest household of young parents with five children. My dad was domineering and made all the financial decisions, which led to years of conflict between my parents. One memory that stood out was a day when my mom bought me a new pair of shoes, only to undergo a harsh reprimand from my father when we got home. I decided early on that I would never "need" anyone's permission. I would be strong, independent, and make my own decisions. I hated feeling weak in any domain of my life. Being a woman in a male-dominated environment only amplified these feelings.

In the midst of this exploration, I remembered another event from my childhood that I hadn't thought of in a long time. I had two younger sisters, and when I was twelve, we all wanted to be competitive gymnasts. Despite knowing we had little money, I begged our parents to enroll us in a local program. After a week of tryouts, I overheard the coach tell my mom he would only accept my two younger sisters because I was "too tall and skinny" and would never become a gymnast. My mom was confused. She had watched the tryouts and thought I was as good as the others. The instructor agreed, but said I "didn't fit the gymnast mold." Sitting there decades later, I vividly recalled feeling fiery anger that someone was telling me I couldn't do something because of an aspect of myself I couldn't control. I burned with a desire to prove him wrong. Furious as well, my mother enrolled all three of us at a gym ninety minutes away, and I went on to compete in gymnastics throughout high school. I knew I got the determination gene from somebody!

The parallels between my childhood and my experience at Encore were startling. The reaction I had when my supervisor spoke to me years ago wasn't accidental. I had felt the pain of being told I wasn't the right fit before. At that moment, it no longer mattered what I wanted—*I had to prove my doubters wrong*. My fierce determination and anger were powerful motivators—but also exhausting. I was overly sensitive to judgments of people in power. If I thought that they didn't believe in my potential, I became competitive, hid my shortcomings, and would stop short of nothing to achieve the necessary results.

When I really took stock, however, the costs of being so guarded were significant. There was a profound gap between who I really was and what I thought I had to be at Encore. I deeply cared about my team. I was passionate about mentoring them and wanted to create a safe learning environment. Instead, I came across as uncaring, judgmental, and not interested in developing people. My need to appear perfect made my team reluctant to bring up issues or mistakes. I was so driven to achieve and succeed that people didn't think they could work for me and have a balanced family life.

These realizations were all the more troubling because I had a secret I didn't dare tell anyone at work. Unbeknownst to my colleagues, my husband and I had been trying to have a baby for many years, including many unsuccessful fertility treatments. I didn't share this very painful, private struggle with anyone because I was sure that if they knew I wanted to be a mother, they wouldn't consider me for the leadership roles I so badly wanted.

I had looked around and done the math: Less than a handful of women had ever held an executive seat at Encore, all with either no or grown children. One woman signed on as SVP of Operations and became pregnant shortly thereafter. She was gone within a year. I never learned why, but I connected dots and drew my own conclusions. Why risk my career growth by sharing my desire to be a mother if becoming one wasn't in the cards for me anyway?

But of course, as fate would have it, within months of receiving this career-defining promotion, I had become pregnant. I had put off telling Brandon, sure that he would have second thoughts if he knew.

Through the feedback and the seminar, I decided I could no longer carry on this facade. My fixation on success came too much at others' expense. I wasn't being the person I wanted to be at work, and I was fed up with these costs to my professional and personal life. What kind of mother would I be if I couldn't let my guard down?

SHAYNE

What we've achieved and where we are in our life today may be the result of clear choices. More often than we realize, however, major life decisions occur by default because of the behavioral reactions of our patterns. As soon as Amy heard, "The CEO was concerned a woman couldn't be effective in this role," there was only one option: "Prove him wrong." Amy's professional trajectory was set by that reaction, not a thoughtful evaluation of her options.

This situation is not specific to Amy. When we look back, we may wonder about the university we attended, the industry we entered, the jobs we took, even which friends we've kept or whom we married. Did we really choose these things because they were what most inspired us? Or did other motivations constrain our sense of possibility and decision-making? Proving others wrong, doing things by default, pleasing our parents or other authority figures, playing it safe, being accepted, doing anything to never be poor again—all are reactions that influence important decisions. Sometimes such decisions turn out for the best; other times they lead us away from what we most want. Proving others wrong may be a powerful motivator, but it puts us at the mercy, and no amount of success will remove the chip from our shoulder. This phenomenon helps explain life crises in which we look around and wonder, "How did I end up here, so unhappy? What am I doing all this for?"

While initially it may be upsetting to recognize unconscious decisions we've made in the past, uncovering these patterns allows us to act differently in the future. Today, if someone were to tell Amy she couldn't do something, hopefully, she'd notice her pinch. By sorting it, she'd realize she is projecting her experience as a twelve-year-old being written off by her gymnastics teacher. She'd recognize the impulse to prove him wrong and know where that leads. She would have the possibility of truly *choosing* what she *actually wants* instead of being driven by rebelling against her doubters.

Another important pattern shaping Amy's life and leadership style was her aversion to feeling or appearing weak. Her pattern of fierce self-reliance fed the competence and resourcefulness that made her a high-performing employee. It helped create her success—*and* it held her back. "No one cared that I was forceful when I was an individual contributor," Amy recalled. "But it became a problem when I led other people. I had hit my 'internal glass ceiling.'"

Let's explore this term. The ego driver to not appear weak or dependent is a gender-blind dreaded image: Both men and women can come across as invulnerable and aggressive. Extensive research indicates, however, that our society is far less forgiving of such traits in women than in men. In addition to receiving a stronger backlash for her aggressive and transactional behavior, Amy was operating in an industry with default preferences for men in certain executive roles. She had to jump through ill-defined additional hoops to obtain the same role as a man, but with a scarcity of women executives to mentor or guide her to her next level. These significant impediments—too often minimized by people who don't face them—contributed to an *external* glass ceiling.

When Amy received her "shocking" 360-degree feedback, she justifiably could have focused on these unfair impediments: "They don't understand; they don't value me because I'm not like them." Or she could have beaten herself up, or shut down and withdrawn.

In doing this, however, she would have missed the gift *for her life*. She wouldn't have discovered the unconscious ways in which she was co-creating stress, pain, and solitude for herself and others. Amy believed she could show no weakness, so she rarely asked for help or feedback, or invited mentoring. Her relationships with peers were guarded transactions instead of partnerships. So, although she excelled at delivering high volumes of work in her zones of competence, she wasn't yet leading down or across the organization.

This was, in her own words, her "internal glass ceiling"—unconscious barriers to success that she herself was erecting. "I wasn't just holding myself and my career back," Amy explained. "In trying to hide my insecurities, I was actually hurting other people. Realizing that was very powerful."

Amy had the courage to move to a learning mindset. By looking inside herself, she gained leverage in a complex situation. "Amy reached a point of being 'fed up' with the costs of her reactions," her coach Carole said. "By letting herself feel sadness about her impact on others, without hedging or deflecting, Amy connected with what *she* deeply wanted to create in her relationships. This clarity became her compass."

When Amy opened up to her team, the results were outstanding. Her work relationships blossomed, and she created a trusting environment where issues were surfaced early and people became a source of support for each other. Her organization's performance, and her effectiveness as a leader, took a leap forward.

The key lay in *why* Amy took the risk of being vulnerable: to mentor others; to leave space for people to grow; to foster openness and honesty. Her sense of purpose allowed her authenticity to create a safe space for her team and deeper connection with people. She was just as committed to delivering results for the organization, but not to prove her worth. "Amy didn't try to be nicer, less assertive, less direct, or less decisive," Carole remarked. "She wasn't willing to sacrifice her competence or performance to appear more likeable. She focused on being more human, vulnerable, and competent *in order to create more authentic connection.*"

But did focusing on her personal responsibility mean pretending there was no external glass ceiling? To the contrary, *self-awareness is the highest act of leadership.* It gives us courage and creates receptiveness in others. Amy's willingness to look at her own limitations gave her tremendous credibility to bring up the discrepancies that women were facing at Encore.

The "How" Makes the "What" Possible

AMY

I felt energized to transform my leadership style and create a positive impact on people around me. I was committed to creating a safe environment so that my team and colleagues could be honest and open with me without feeling judged or criticized. To do this, I needed to show more of my human side: to be vulnerable, to ask for help, and to let others know my fears and anxieties. Most of all, I wanted to share more of my world—to let people in.

It felt great . . . but the first step was telling Brandon I was pregnant. The LaL seminar had a number of role-play exercises where we practiced difficult conversations. I did all of mine on the conversation I needed to have with Brandon. I rehearsed it again on the way to the office my first day back at work. I was ready.

I walked into his office, fully prepared to have a poised dialogue, sat down, and . . . started crying. *This is not the plan!* Through my tears, I managed to spit out the words "I'm pregnant."

"Congratulations!" Brandon exclaimed. "That's amazing! But why are you upset?" Even through my blurry vision I could see the confusion on his face.

"I don't know how this is going to impact my career," I told him, trying to regain my composure. "I know you just promoted me, but I promise you this won't impact my performance. I've got everything under control."

"What are you talking about?" he said. "I have no doubt your performance will be fine. And no, you may not have everything under control, and that's OK. We'll figure this out together."

"I've already decided I only need two months' maternity leave," I said, knowing he must be worried about me being absent, and Encore not being able to purchase enough portfolio. *Don't take this away from me!* "I'll be back before you know it."

"Stop worrying, Amy. This is your first baby. You have no idea how much time you'll need. Please promise me that you'll figure that out as it goes, and ask me for help."

I nodded, feeling stunned.

He stood up and gave me a hug. I couldn't remember Brandon ever hugging me before. It was the first time I felt a personal connection with him.

Now that my secret was out, I used it as an offering to my team. I shared my story; my fears, anxieties, and goals. I wasn't sure what to expect, but I quickly saw evidence that being vulnerable and authentic had a positive impact on others. My team began telling me what was going on in their personal lives, which made our relationships more meaningful. From a performance perspective, I had been begging them for years to tell me any bad news early so we could deal with it proactively. When I showed my humanity, we started building trust and it finally happened. As a group, we began to get ahead of problems more consistently.

One cloud of frustration still hung over me. It was customary for vice president promotions to be announced to the entire company. When Brandon gave me the VP role, however, he mentioned waiting a little before making it public. Weeks became a month, and then several months. The longer it went on, the more I lost my courage to ask him about it. I was afraid what I might hear. *Maybe I'm on trial, or maybe Brandon is hearing from the board or other executives that I can't handle the job after all.* I had worked so incredibly hard to get to this point, and now I felt deflated. I was the only woman on the executive team, except I wasn't "officially" a full member. When my promotion was finally announced with all the other annual promotions six months later, it was a non-event.

I worked through my feelings with Carole and didn't let it derail my focus. I continued to share my fears and my experiences with my team and others. I noticed how this broke the cycle of fear and judgment and instead generated understanding, learning, and connection. Dramatic change happened. Only the deeper tensions and struggles I felt as a woman at Encore stayed bottled up. They felt too raw and dangerous to divulge. I knew, however, that these fears and beliefs would limit me. At some point, I needed to resolve these issues.

Part of what I learned at LaL was the importance of telling authentic stories of change. In the safe setting of my next seminar, I shared my uncensored story for the first time. I couldn't believe the positive response I received from the other participants. Afterward, Shayne pulled me aside and urged me to share my story with Brandon.

When I returned to the office, I took what seemed like the ultimate risk. I walked Brandon through my experience as a woman at Encore: the comments, the missed promotions, and my questions about titles and compensation. I did my best to separate my interpretation of each event from the facts and circumstances. I also told him what I saw as my part: not asking questions, being afraid to know, being guarded.

To my surprise, Brandon just listened. It was the first time he had heard about any of this, and he didn't try to explain or justify.

"I totally get how you felt," he said. When we talked about not announcing my promotion to VP, he was upset by how I'd experienced it. "I was getting pushback from the leadership team on intra-cycle promotions, and I had just agreed not to do any more outside of our formal processes in February and September. We made your change in March, and if I'm honest, I optimized for myself. I didn't want to deal with the team telling me I'd violated an agreement we'd just made.

"I didn't stop to think about it from your perspective. Honestly, it never occurred to me that anyone would doubt that the position was really yours. Also, while I knew we had an underrepresentation of women in senior management, I didn't equate that to a broader gender diversity problem. I'm disappointed that this could be seen as another example of a lack of recognition for women at Encore. I totally missed that, and I'm sorry."

We discussed what else had been going on during each of the incidents. His openness really helped debunk my conclusions. Something also seemed to click for Brandon. We talked about the perception gap between men and women at Encore, and how similar things might be holding other women back. We began bouncing around the idea of a diversity initiative. Neither of us knew what that would look like or where to start, but it was exciting. I wanted to improve the experience of women at Encore. I wanted people to help other Encore employees feel safe about being authentic in their leadership in a way I hadn't let myself be for years.

Brandon and I decided to let things evolve naturally, but the following year, at our annual management conference, it was painfully obvious that we needed to do something more proactive. Now a senior vice president, I was the only woman at that level. Of the twenty-five leaders in the room, only two were women.

Brandon noticed too. "It's obvious we're not making progress on our overall diversity," he said. "We've talked about it in prior meetings, and I thought it would change organically. It hasn't, and we need to figure out why. Amy, I need you to lead a diversity initiative."

At first I felt annoyed. *Of course, he is asking the only female executive to run the diversity initiative.* Nonetheless, what choice did I have? Noticing my pinch, I thought about the ways in which my fear of being judged or appearing weak had held me back. There were external barriers to my success, but I needed to break through my own internal glass ceiling to increase my influence within the organization. Brandon was offering me the opportunity to help others succeed.

"I'll do it," I told him.

That was the easy part. Despite the fact that I was a woman, I didn't know anything about promoting diversity. *Where do I start?* For the next couple of months, I explored ideas and worked to identify Encore's specific opportunities. I met with diversity scholars, who eventually convinced me that a good start would be addressing the specific challenges women faced in our organization. Women@Encore, Encore's Women's Leadership Program, was born. An essential part of the program was to help women recognize both their internal glass ceilings and the external ones—and to give them the tools and insights necessary to begin to dismantle both.

The experiences and developmental opportunities we created are among my proudest professional accomplishments. I cherished this work even as I often put it aside for the high-pressure demands of leading Business Development. Progress was slow; some days I felt great hope, others great frustration. But wherever I could, I worked to bring these internal and external barriers to light.

SHAYNE

Learning as Leadership was cofounded by Claire Nuer. I want to briefly refer to her life in order to illustrate one of her most important insights in creating this methodology.

Claire was born Jewish in France in 1933. She was a hidden child, experienced persecution and separation, and lost her father in Auschwitz. After the liberation, she became a feisty young woman who was committed to righting all wrongs and fighting all injustices. She demonstrated, signed petitions, and decried anyone who didn't "get it." She angrily fought any bias or inequality through blaming and shaming "the bad guys." Because she believed herself to be *just and righteous*, the end justified the means.

Later in life, Claire came to a stunning and upsetting realization. She had suffered from aggression and hatred during the war. But her antagonistic behavior after the war reproduced similar dynamics of conflict, animosity, and incomprehension. Ultimately, she decided that the most important goal was not to right all wrongs, but rather to create an environment where people could learn to be better human beings. Being direct and clear was imperative, but that became destructive without empathy and respect. She realized that *the "space" in which we raise issues matters as much as the content does.*

Claire decided to stop perpetuating "warlike" environments with her behavior. By fostering dialogue and mutual understanding, instead of fear, she learned to inspire people to raise their consciousness, and in doing so she became a more effective change agent and person.

Amy's journey offers an instructive example of this lesson. She reached the most senior roles at Encore and challenged the status quo for other women and minorities—all without alienating the leaders and staff. Amy's biggest obstacle was learning to openly raise her concerns. If, like the younger Claire, Amy had stormed into Brandon's office to tell him Encore had a diversity issue or that he didn't treat women equitably, it probably wouldn't have ended well. "I have a desired image of being 'super inclusive,'" Brandon said. "If Amy had told me I was biased, I would have given her the ten reasons why she was wrong." Amy and Brandon would likely have ended up in a heated debate over who had the higher moral ground.

If Amy had raised her concerns in a productive way and Brandon dismissed her, she would have felt distressed. Such a negative reaction by Brandon, as an authority figure, would have conveyed to Amy that her experience wasn't welcome at Encore. So the space in which Brandon responded mattered if he hoped to create a transparent, fully engaged culture.

In all of this, Amy, through *the quality of her goal*, had a lot more "power" and influence than she realized. She wasn't aiming to be vindicated, to extract an apology, or to impose a specific solution she knew was best. Her intention was to create a more authentic relationship with

Brandon and to learn from her experiences. Amy took the risk of sharing her perceptions, despite her fears that doing so would damage their relationship and limit her career growth inside the organization.

Amy—and Brandon in his response—also embodied the five core aspects of constructive communication: being vulnerable, empathetic, direct, exploratory, and caring (VEDEC). Amy shared her experiences in plain, direct, and personal terms. Such specificity was more uncomfortable than making intellectual or general statements, but her vulnerability made Brandon stop and listen more carefully and with more empathy. "I could tell what she was saying was really important to her," he remembered.

Amy also kept an exploratory mindset, knowing that her experience might not be the whole reality. This allowed Brandon to feel safe enough to search for his blind spots rather than defend his integrity. His vulnerable admissions—namely, that he hadn't considered how Amy, as a woman, might internalize some of his decisions, or whether he might have promoted a man more quickly—helped Amy see him as genuine and open-minded. Later, when Brandon described factors she wasn't aware of, she didn't take it as defensive or justifying. She felt empathy for the complications of his position and was able to assimilate these elements into a fuller sense of reality.

Unfortunately, our egosystem too often uses our feelings of caring for others as an excuse *not* to talk as opposed to providing motivation for *how* we talk. Amy and Brandon cared about each other as people, not just colleagues, and this intention to support and make each other good was infused throughout their discussions about this topic.

There are no guarantees in life. No matter how effectively Amy broached her experience of being a woman at Encore, Brandon could have reacted unfavorably. But Amy's simple, nonjudgmental vulnerability gave her the greatest chance of helping Brandon to see Encore through her eyes. Brandon's willingness to listen without judgment or defensiveness allowed him to connect dots that changed the way he saw the world and inspired him to address an issue—how gender manifested itself in his company—that many executives would have shied away from.

When we work on our ego triggers, any conversation becomes possible. Instead of treacherous conflicts, even discussions of race, gender, or other charged topics can be starting points of connection, growth, and concrete change.

BRANDON

My conversations with Amy were some of the most impactful moments in my career. Her trepidation at telling me she was pregnant made me question many things, including how well I knew my team. I had other direct reports who were more reserved, and I thought they might be reticent about sharing personal news, but I was sure I knew Amy. *I must have no clue about what it feels like to be a woman in the workplace!* I thought. This experience, coupled with our many other conversations, helped me see Encore through a different lens. I'm eternally grateful for Amy's authenticity.

Initially, I didn't act on a broad diversity program because I thought being aware of the issue was enough. None of us were ill intended, and we were working hard to become a more conscious and empathetic culture. I expected it to naturally evolve in the right direction. Several years later, however, the under-representation on both the U.S. and Indian management teams was the same. I realized that if we didn't make it a corporate-wide priority, it would never change.

Beyond Women@Encore, I took away something more important from Amy's journey. Until then, I saw a sexist as a character out of *Mad*

Men. I now realize how unconscious and invisible my biases and blind spots are. There is a lot for us as leaders, especially white men, to learn about the unwanted impacts our behaviors have on different groups. I can't promise I'll always see them, but I will be looking and hopefully gaining a broader view by relying on the perspectives of a diverse cadre of individuals.

CHAPTER 8

"THOSE" PEOPLE HAVE SOMETHING IMPORTANT TO TEACH YOU

———

Even the Boss Feels Powerless

BRANDON

In late August 2009, George Lund and I were having dinner with some of Encore's outside advisers on the terrace at Mr. A's in downtown San Diego. We were taking in the views of Coronado and the aircraft carrier USS *Midway* and watching planes land at Lindbergh Field when my phone rang. It was my general counsel. He asked me to take the call, so I excused myself and stepped away from the table.

"A judge in Ohio has ruled our collection affidavit insufficient and ordered it to be amended immediately," he told me. "We need to change the document prior to putting it back into production."

"Sounds simple. Let's get it in place," I interrupted him mid-sentence, wanting to get back to my dinner guests. "Thanks for the call."

"I don't think you understand, Brandon. It may sound simple, but it's not. We have to immediately recall all the affidavits being used around the country and re-create our entire process. We can't produce or use another affidavit until it's completed."

Debt collection is a fairly simple business from a process perspective. We have three ways to contact people: make a phone call, send a letter, and initiate litigation. The advent of smartphones made our calls increasingly less effective because our customers could easily ignore them. If a consumer also failed to respond to our letters, our sole remaining option was legal action. It's an expensive last resort, so we used it only when we believed an individual had the ability to pay but was just ignoring us. Our outside law firms relied on affidavits—legal documents that established the fundamental facts of our relationship with the customer and our right to pursue collection. It was an essential piece of the process. Without it, obtaining remedies from the court would be extremely difficult.

"That seems drastic. It's just changing some paperwork. Can't we appeal?"

"No. Even though the changes are only procedural, we can't knowingly file another affidavit until it's fixed."

I sighed. "OK, shut down the presses. I'll call a meeting first thing tomorrow. We'll scope out the problem and figure out a plan."

On my ride home, I called Paul. Addressing this problem would require a wholesale redistribution of resources. Our legal and project management teams would need to immediately redesign the process and create business requirements. All software development projects had to be stopped so programmers could focus on making these changes. Added to that, there were dozens of law firms who collected on our behalf that needed to be briefed. While the new system would take some time to implement, these meetings needed to happen in the next few days to ensure that no affidavits remained in production.

The next morning, as I briefed the entire leadership team, the conversation naturally focused on identifying solutions and the need for quick, coordinated action. I listened to them, marveling at how different this discussion was from past crises. There was no griping or resistance, and not even a hint of trying to figure out who was to blame. We had a problem to solve, and all our collective energy drove it to conclusion.

I was delighted by the result. It took just ninety days to completely reengineer the process and train our law firms. This quick action kept the company from missing any financial targets.

The affidavit crisis behind us, we headed into 2010 with significant momentum. Our performance was robust, with most financial metrics increasing 25 percent year over year. We continued to see reduced competition and an abundant flow of new portfolio purchases at very attractive pricing levels. Morale was high, the stock price continued to rise, and the contributions from India were meaningfully driving down our costs.

Only the regulatory and legislative pressures emerging from the 2008 recession tempered my enthusiasm. The general public increasingly believed that corporate greed was responsible for the economic downturn and that certain industries should be held accountable. There was particular animosity toward all financial institutions, not just banks. If you lent money or provided services to those companies, you were in the hot seat. I empathized with the anger about the meltdown and the need for targeted regulation. At the same time, I worried that the government, feeling pressured to take action, would push impractical measures.

In January I met with a good friend of mine, Greg Koch, who is the cofounder and CEO of Stone Brewing Co. He and I were in the same YPO chapter, a group that brought together disparate business owners and CEOs. Greg was known for his consumer advocate leanings and was helping me prepare a presentation about Encore for our YPO Forum. I wanted the Forum's advice on navigating through the forthcoming regulatory challenges.

"There's so much negative emotion right now," I told Greg. "The facts are getting lost or distorted. The word 'debt' has such a negative connotation."

"Why don't you do something about it?" asked Greg.

"I'd love to find a way to distance ourselves from these perceptions, but I haven't been able to cut through the noise."

"Why don't you create the kind of company that customers will want to do business with rather than avoid? Who says there can't be a model debt collection company?"

"How many beers have you had today? We're building a great company for our employees and shareholders, but we collect debt! We're not making beer or selling organic food. Our customers can't choose us, and there's definitely nothing exciting about our service."

"I understand, Brandon, but you said people often owe several different companies. So they *do* have a choice about whom they pay. That could be the place of emphasis for you. Think outside the box. Stop being so negative!"

I sat back, staring at him intently. Although many people think poorly of debt collection, I felt at peace with our work and how we conducted ourselves. We were an inglorious necessity. If no mechanism were in place to guarantee that people paid back the money they borrowed, credit would either be too expensive or nonexistent. Our current financial system simply wouldn't work. Years earlier, I had committed myself to connecting each employee to the essential service we provide society. I believed that without reservation.

On the other hand, I also had concluded it was impossible to have an inspiring mission that would resonate with Encore's employees and consumers. It would be so much easier to build a great company if we cured cancer, developed new technologies, or even just brewed bold craft beer. Instead, we were in a notorious industry doing a job few people wanted to do. *Easy for Greg to say I should think outside the box.*

SHAYNE

Brandon and his team had seemingly reached the pinnacle of organizational transformation. The performance results, the effective crisis management, the empowered workforce—Encore was firing on all cylinders. But his conversation with Greg Koch resurfaced a nagging dissatisfaction. No matter how great a corporate culture they created, Encore was still stuck doing the dirty work of society. There seemed no way out of this trap.

Such feelings of ambivalence existed more broadly in Encore. During our first WeLead program at Encore in 2007, a senior leader asked in frustration, "How can I have an inspiring 'at the source' goal when I sue people for a living?"

Many of us hold a common assumption that certain companies clearly have a meaningful mission and others do not. Many leaders working in industries without redeeming social values feel ambivalent and find themselves just doing their job for the paycheck or because they have no other options.

Brandon had resolved this in his mind. He didn't see himself as evil for leading a debt collection firm—but he had resigned himself to working in an industry where few people connected emotionally with its societal value. This is in part because he felt trapped by the larger system in which Encore operated. In our complex, diverse society, it is easy to feel like a tiny cog in a big machine. If we litter occasionally, what's the big deal? Our one vote doesn't really matter, does it? This feeling of insignificance often affects how we view our role in larger problems. What can any one of us really do about homelessness, income inequality, or climate change? Author and organizational development pioneer Peter Senge often asks the question "How is it that we collectively create outcomes none of us want?"

This was the case in Encore's industry. Who, in fact, could affect the debt collection system? Consumers? Caught in a cycle of debt, they undoubtedly felt voiceless. Encore's employees? The call center employees contacting consumers often saw themselves merely as worker bees. They had limited, if any, influence. Their bosses in middle management believed the executive team held the power. Moving up, the executive team felt like the CEO called the shots. If anyone could make change happen, it was Brandon.

And yet Brandon, CEO of one of the largest companies in his industry, felt he had little influence over how the industry operated, was perceived, or fit into the larger financial system. He had to answer to the board and deliver results for the shareholders. If he stopped performing, his position would quickly become precarious.

So, is it the chairman of the board who has the power to make things different? He or she can only give guidance and hold management accountable. The shareholders—whom management often fears displeasing or letting down—typically feel like outsiders. They can complain, but they don't really have a say in how the company is run or impacts society. An individual legislator can't pass laws on his or her own, and anyway, regulators are overextended enforcing the existing set of laws.

This is not to say that we all have the same amount of influence; rather, this highlights our ubiquitous feeling of powerlessness in broader problems. Most of us believe that someone else higher up in the chain could do something, but not us.

Amy certainly didn't think she could influence Encore's unconscious attitudes toward women. But when she took the risk to share her experience, she discovered she had far more power and influence than she realized. She didn't do this alone—her coach supported her, Brandon listened to her, and outside resources guided her—*but it could never have happened without her.*

Within Encore, Brandon and Amy had the authority to make change. Brandon had no such clout in the broader industry, however—or did he? Could awareness of his own egosystem help him access possibilities that usually remain hidden?

Taking Responsibility for My Part, No Matter What

BRANDON

On our quarterly earnings calls with analysts and shareholders, we would discuss our financial performance, provide context for our results, and answer questions. It was our practice to never offer any guidance or speculation. Once a year, however, we held Encore's Investor Day, where we offered our thoughts on trends and future possibilities. The meeting was usually held in New York City in early June, and every shareholder was invited, along with analysts and bankers. It was an important event, and we spent a great deal of time preparing for it.

Several weeks before the 2010 meeting, a report was released by a coalition of nonprofit organizations that provided services to lower-income residents in New York. They took issue with the business model of companies like Encore and accused the industry of systematically trying to collect from individuals with no ability to pay. After a quick review, I dismissed the report and its authors. Their findings were inconsistent with our processes and accused us of using practices that made no finan-cial sense. The last thing we wanted was to initiate collection activity if a customer couldn't pay. Besides harming our reputation, it wouldn't be profitable. I knew we wouldn't win the moral argument, but I figured the report would go away as quickly as it arrived.

Wrong again. The report gained traction in the media, and I grew outraged that these local nonprofits were getting national attention without having to defend their accusations. Newspaper after newspaper picked up the story without checking to see if the claims were accurate. Internally, our Decision Science team took the initiative to investigate the report's conclusions. Their analysis showed the statistical method-ology used was flawed and they began writing a white paper outlining the findings.

Despite that, I was still furious. "Can you believe they had the gall to take public shots at our industry without having the decency to call us first?" I vented to Dana that night. "We're finalizing a report that dis-credits their methodology. They picked a fight with the wrong company."

"Are you really surprised they didn't contact you directly?" she asked me. "Would you have actually taken the time to talk with them if they had?"

"With reports like this, they wouldn't deserve my time."

"Are you sure they don't have a point? Maybe these people care deeply about their cause and just want to be heard. For all we know, they've already tried and you ignored them. In any case, I doubt they're 100 percent wrong."

Dana's disagreement caused me to stop and consider my reaction. She had been volunteering at a few nonprofits and had enrolled in a master's degree program for nonprofit leadership at the University of San Diego. Her challenging response helped highlight for me that I was pinched, plain and simple. Putting aside my angry mind chatter about how inaccurate the report's accusations were, I identified how my ego was taking it personally. I had interpreted the report as a public attack on my character. I was Satan preying on the weak and poor—at its most basic, a bad person. Understanding this deflated my emotion, and I reluctantly reconsidered Dana's perspective. I didn't know if she was right, but the last thing I wanted was to openly discredit these organizations. They didn't need additional reasons to rally against our industry. The white paper would stay within Encore.

I refocused my energy on preparing for our Investor Day on June 9. If any analysts or shareholders asked questions at the meeting, I'd set the record straight. The negative news reports had stopped, so I figured the issue was finally behind us. Then, on the morning of June 8, my general counsel pulled me aside. He had received a call that the authors of the report were planning on attending our meeting.

"Should we get extra security for the ballroom?" he asked. "They're only entitled to attend if they are Encore shareholders. If so, we have to let them in. If not, we can kick them out."

My anger about the report was long gone. Dana had helped me see I might've been overreacting. I still didn't agree with the conclusions, but if they came, they would find a welcome audience. "Honestly," I said, "I don't think they'll actually show."

The meeting was scheduled to start at 8:30 am in the upstairs ballroom of Le Parker Méridien on West 57th Street. The elevator banks of the hotel overlook Central Park. The view is spectacular, and it gave me plenty of inspiration for the day. Encore was doing phenomenally well, and I couldn't wait to tell our story. I went to the ballroom thirty minutes early to greet people as they arrived, but the room was already 90 percent full with our shareholders, board of directors, analysts, and bankers.

I walked around the room, somewhat anxiously, and just before George Lund called the meeting to order, unfamiliar faces arrived at the sign-in desk. They showed up after all!

My general counsel asked if I still wanted to let them in.

"Of course." I nodded.

They registered and looked for available seats. The only open spots were directly in front of the podium. Normally you put a friendly face up front to give the speaker positive reinforcement. Not today.

I thought back to my conversation with Greg Koch. Was there a way for us to create a better company by seeking these individuals' input?

George, Paul, and I each went through our parts of the presentation and then opened up the floor to questions. It's an interesting dance between people who run public companies and analysts who give advice to the public about whether to buy or sell a company's stock. The analysts ask questions and then examine your tone and every word of your response, hoping to glean something that signaled whether the stock was likely to go up or down. As an executive, you attempt to answer their questions while only revealing what's been disclosed previously. I was pretty good at it by this point.

I was about to close the meeting after twenty minutes of Q&A when one of the individuals from the nonprofits raised her hand. She introduced herself and her colleagues and their affiliation to the recently drafted report. She reiterated many of the predatory practices outlined in the report, declaring several times that we targeted the poor and underprivileged. I believe she actually said, "You are awful people and should be ashamed of what you do for a living."

After what felt like five minutes, she concluded, "Are you prepared to admit your involvement in these terrible practices and change them immediately?"

To my surprise, I was neither mad nor embarrassed. I was thinking instead how frustrating it must be to have to come to a public forum and shout at somebody just to be heard. She was obviously a bright woman who was convinced I was leading a company doing something very wrong. I knew that most of what she said wasn't true. So where was her anger coming from?

"Thank you," I said. "While I completely disagree with the substance of your allegations, I would like to meet with you to understand your perspective and to see if we can open the lines of communication."

I reached into my pocket and handed her a business card. She and her colleagues each gave me theirs, and I promised to be in contact within a week. I adjourned the meeting.

After they left, many people came up to tell me how pissed they were at the group and how well I handled the situation.

"Who do they think they are?" asked several participants.

"What gives them the right to come in here and accuse you of anything?" said others. "Why would anybody view them credibly?"

Those who reacted most negatively thought my business card gesture was a brilliant ruse to get them out of the room. Almost everybody assumed I wouldn't call and that there would be no meeting. Except for my management team—they knew I was serious and most volunteered to attend.

SHAYNE

The destructive ego dynamics Encore Capital Group eliminated from its culture can be readily found in the public sphere. Arguing over who is right, making others bad, ignoring how our own behavior perpetuates the gridlock—all of this fuels many of our most polarized issues. From liberal vs. conservative and business vs. environment, to Main Street vs. Wall Street and black vs. white, we often square off on opposite sides of a dispute, convinced the other side just doesn't "get it," without realizing that we are participating in a very predictable Us vs. Them dysfunction.

Although these are sprawling social conflicts, the leaders arguing about them are still just . . . people. They exhibit the same ego triggers and self-fulfilling prophecy behaviors previously dissected between Dave and Brandon or between Finance and Operations.

Encore faced these larger dynamics because of the industry it operated in. Our norms and political views often cause us to decry certain industries as being harmful: fossil fuels, banking, weapons, government regulation, lobbying, and environmental activism, to name a few. Employees in these industries may or may not perceive a higher purpose, but people at the other end of the political spectrum often prescribe ill intent to them. We forget they are ordinary people just like ourselves, with aspirations, fears, egos, and dysfunctions. They aren't bad people because they do what they do. On the other hand, *how* they do it does have consequences.

Brandon and his team, bolstered by the white paper, initially reacted by summarily dismissing the report released by the coalition of nonprofits. You might even notice which group you identify with. If you are more business oriented, you may feel antipathy toward social justice or environmental activists and easily see them as aggressive, close-minded, or holier than thou. If you are more of an activist, you may notice your own set of conclusions about people in big business: selfish, arrogant, willing to sacrifice the larger good to line their own pockets.

Any time we feel this animosity toward another group, it is a sign that we are making them bad through the prism of our judgments. The nonprofits believed that Encore's business practices were predatory, and Brandon needed to be held accountable. Phrases like "You should be ashamed of what you do for a living," however, led Brandon to believe his integrity and character were being assaulted. If he hadn't sorted his pinch ahead of time, he would have just lashed out to defend his honor. The coalition's concerns about the people struggling in the financial system would have become lost in the escalation. Amy's story illustrated how the "space" in which we communicate makes the content possible. Inversely, blaming and accusing makes the possibility of dialogue nearly impossible. Every time leaders on one side of a conflict behave in ways that trigger the other's fight–flight reactions, *they help to perpetuate the very problem they want so badly to resolve.*

But something fundamental had changed in Brandon over the previous five years. He had seen time and again the destruction that being right and making bad produced inside Encore and knew that nothing useful emerged from perpetuating these dynamics. And so, when he found himself in the crosshairs of a societal Us vs. Them, he took a stand. Not for his point of view or righteous certainty on the subject, but for what he, as a leader of significant power, *would no longer perpetuate through his own behavior.*

This is another example of a never again. Brandon didn't have a strategy for how to respond at the Investor Day meeting. But his clarity that he would not prolong dysfunction and distrust dictated what he would *not* let himself do. As leaders and citizens of the planet, our never again is our own line in the sand. No matter what we perceive others are doing, we are responsible for how we behave and the impact we have.

In fact, it is precisely when we believe others are making *us* bad that we most need our commitment to make *them* good. We are the last hope in that moment to create progress instead of regress. This challenge is not intellectual—it is visceral and experiential. Ninety-nine percent of us prioritize our ego's sense of self-worth 99 percent of the time. In this instance, Brandon took a different path, one of curiosity, learning, even care. He reached across the divide instead of succumbing to the easy, seductive habit of being right.

Such acts of leadership matter because the consequences of our societal breakdowns are more far-reaching than our organizational ones are. If leaders of consumer protection organizations cannot productively talk with financial services leaders, the lives of the people they are trying to protect will not improve. Encore's industry, for example, will continue to have a poor reputation, making it ripe for bad press and restrictive legislation. The U.S. economy will bear the weight of millions of people struggling to become solvent. Everyone loses. This same dynamic plays out in other industries: oil and gas, with the controversy over fracking; real estate development and environmentalists; banking and regulators; Congress. People on all sides make their counterparts bad, encouraging— almost ensuring that—the other side reacts in kind. Broadly speaking, as a society, we choose being right over making progress.

When Brandon transcended his self-worth drivers, his leadership perspective didn't become altruistic, but rather *comprehensive*. A financial CEO can think about profit *and* the consumer. An oil and gas executive can push for peak production *and* care about the environment. I've seen it. A government policy maker can hold banks accountable *and* support a fluid business environment. It is our triggered egos and entrenched Us vs. Them dynamics that propel us into extreme positions.

A Rock Can Change the Course of a River

BRANDON

The following week I called Jim, the executive director of one of the nonprofits in the coalition. He sounded surprised to hear from me, but he agreed to contact the other coalition members. We scheduled a meeting for early July.

I was both excited and apprehensive. I would be having a conversation with people who seemed to hate me—while key people on my own team continued to insist these nonprofits were untrustworthy. The danger that we would all escalate into an argument, or worse, was high. For anything useful to happen, my hot buttons could not get pushed. I talked the situation over with Shayne, and he asked me what my goals were for the meeting.

"I want to clear up where their venom comes from," I said. "Their anger doesn't make sense to me."

"Do you mean you're hoping to show them you're a team of good people and they shouldn't be frustrated?" he asked.

I saw right away what he meant. If I tried to politely point out where their beliefs were off base, we wouldn't get very far.

"If we put aside your integrity and reputation, and who's right or wrong, what are your true goals in meeting with them? What are your intentions *for* them?"

I paused, searching for what was really at stake in this meeting. "We've done focus groups to try to see what the collections process feels like from our consumers' vantage point. But there's still a gap, or these activists wouldn't be so riled up. I really want to learn from this group. What do they see that we don't?"

Something deeper was coming to the surface as I talked. "I'm so tired of all this fighting," I told Shayne. "The anger. Judging each other. It doesn't have to be this way. Even if nothing concrete comes from our time together, I want to create a human connection with them."

I flew to New York with four executives, including our vice president of Legal Collections, Ashish Masih. We met in a conference room at the same hotel as on Investor Day. The Encore team sat on one side of a long rectangular table, while six leaders from the nonprofit coalition sat on the other.

My team and I introduced ourselves. We each shared some background on who we were and what we did. When it was their turn, the leaders of the nonprofits in the coalition stated their name and organizational affiliation. They offered no additional details, conjuring up an image of soldiers captured in hostile territory. I took a deep breath then began, hoping to set a productive tone for the meeting.

"I am grateful that you took the time to come today. I don't know what to expect in terms of outcomes, but I do want you to know that we're committed to having an open dialogue. There's a lot of emotion on both sides of this issue. I know you have a negative view of our company and believe we target your constituents. At the same time, I personally took offense to your conclusions. It felt like you were indicting my character and that of our entire workforce. I hope to be able to keep those emotions at bay throughout the day. If you ever feel judged or dismissed by anything I say, please let me know. Quite simply, our goal is to learn what is driving your beliefs about us and to begin an ongoing relationship."

I paused. They nodded their heads but didn't add anything. We were all trying to appear relaxed, but the atmosphere was tense. There was no road map for such a conversation. After ten long seconds of silence, I continued.

"Let's start by seeing if we have any common ground. My first question is whether we agree that someone who borrows money should pay it back if they have the means."

They looked at each other, then one of them answered cautiously, "Yes, but that's not your business model."

"One step at a time," I said. "So, if we are aligned on that, I'd like to review how Encore makes money. It may sound trivial, but if we can all agree on the basic math, it should make the other discussions less emotionally charged."

"What do you mean by 'basic math'?" one of them asked. I thought she sounded annoyed. *Did basic math sound condescending?* I needed to be more vigilant with my choice of words.

"Well, if your constituents only make enough money to pay for food and rent, they certainly can't afford to pay us anything," I explained. "Given that, there is no incentive for us to try to contact them. We would just lose money."

"Companies like yours just call everybody and hope that your threats scare people into paying," Jim responded.

That was both wrong and insulting. I resisted the urge to tell him that their report and analytical skills were hopelessly flawed. *It's just a pinch.* I took another deep breath. *My goal is to connect with them and understand their perspective.*

"I understand that's your perception," I said, "but if we did that, we'd go out of business. Factually, over the lifetime of a portfolio, 80 percent of our consumers pay us *nothing*. In any given month, we receive payments from less than 1 percent of our consumers. If we expended energy on the 99 percent that don't pay us each month, we would go broke. This is not a business where you can indiscriminately apply effort. We have spent tens of millions of dollars acquiring and analyzing information to identify who can and who cannot pay."

"Are you claiming with 100 percent accuracy that you don't call people who are poor and unable to pay?" one of the other nonprofit coalition leaders asked.

Really? The "100%" test? I felt my face flushing. It was like the shareholder meeting all over again, and I was being told to admit we were terrible people. Perhaps sensing I was going to say something flippant, Ashish answered the question.

"Not at all," he said. "I am sure we make mistakes. But it isn't our intent, and we would stop collection activity if we were aware of it.

Unfortunately, we rarely get phone calls from our customers so we can't appreciate their individual circumstances."

"Well, we've spoken to your customers," Jim stated, "and they have a lot to say."

This is why we're here, I told myself. *Learn, don't defend.*

The nonprofit coalition had identified consumers who had been contacted by our company. We reviewed each case together thoroughly. While there was no pattern of targeting, I was surprised to discover several important process inefficiencies in the overall collection system. For example, the transfer of ownership from the original creditor to companies like Encore caused a lot of confusion. The bank wasn't required to send a letter to the individual, so the only communication came from the collection company. Most consumers didn't recognize our name and some concluded it was some sort of scam. There were three or four examples like this, each with a reasonable explanation. The coalition had concluded that these process inefficiencies were intentional. I had requested this meeting out of curiosity, but I was beginning to understand how unaware consumers were of what was happening with their account. We were unearthing things that could actually improve the process for everybody.

"While we hear your answers," Jim said, "it doesn't explain one fundamental question." His face said he was still suspicious and clearly dissatisfied. "How could every customer we encounter have a problem but there not be a systematic attempt by Encore to mislead people?"

I paused, realizing our conversation wasn't about a series of individual discrepancies. To them, the sheer volume of evidence pointed to us doing this intentionally. Looking at it through their eyes, their conclusions did seem self-evident. I felt a wave of empathy. I would believe the same thing!

How could this perception gap be so drastic? "You have to understand," I began, working it out as I spoke, "Encore works with over 10 million customers. If our models were 99 percent accurate, we would still contact 100,000 people who were unable to pay. If 10 percent of those sought the guidance of a local nonprofit office, that would be 10,000 people. Through our lens, we are incredibly precise, but I totally understand how, seen through yours, we are systematically targeting thousands of impoverished people."

I was going to stop there but I wanted to do more than hide behind numbers, even if it felt vulnerable to admit. "As Ashish pointed out, our models aren't perfect and we certainly make mistakes. But I promise you that we are not heartless. We're doing the best we can inside an enormous system."

"Consumers just don't know what to expect," responded one of the coalition members. Her tone was calmer. "The laws governing your industry aren't clear and don't detail how people can reach out and challenge the information you have. They're paralyzed by fear. What are you doing to make it clearer for them? What makes you different?"

She wasn't trying to criticize or corner us with this question. It was a genuine inquiry. The answer was that we weren't doing anything specific to separate ourselves. We complied with the laws, which were admittedly archaic. As evident as it now sounded, it hadn't occurred to me to expand upon these rules to create clarity for our consumers.

By the end of the day, we seemed to be finally hearing each other, even building on each other. I asked if they were open to further discussions, and to my surprise, they were. I felt a tiny hope that together we might be able to create meaningful change.

After they left, our team reviewed the day. The conversations had given us a deeper sense of the overwhelming fear and confusion many of our consumers felt. We felt inspired to engage with them differently and to separate ourselves from the historical view and practices of our industry.

My friend Greg was right. There was an opportunity to create a company that consumers would want to work with.

SHAYNE

If, to stop perpetuating the Us vs. Them dynamics, Brandon refused to be dominated by defending or proving his self-worth, what could his compass be instead?

Brandon consciously set goals for the meeting with the nonprofit leaders of "creating a human connection" and "truly understanding their perspective." Viewed through the lens of how we typically interact with opposing social groups, these intentions seem virtuous—but crazy. In Brandon's shoes, we would enter such a meeting with the goal of *winning* the discussion through being right. Any acknowledgment of the other side's perspective would be lost points in a negotiation.

We've talked previously about the power and importance of identifying our true goals in shifting out of our dysfunctions. Whatever mindset we choose will be instrumental to our behavior and the outcomes of any conversation. When we are motivated by learning, connecting with others, and contributing to something larger, our self-worth tension subsides. We feel more inspired, purpose driven, and connected. In Brandon's case, this approach opened doors to outcomes that would have otherwise been nearly impossible.

Brandon's goals were not "shoulds"; rather, they were his deep intentions that mattered more to him than did defending his character. He was committed, moment by moment, to a different direction. And when he lost his center, Ashish stepped in, highlighting how creating change is a team effort.

Brandon's decision to engage the nonprofit leaders was unusual. Most executives in the power position of such a conflict prefer to ignore or discredit their critics. Why would anybody put himself in such an uncomfortable, no-win situation? And yet, this peculiar decision was self-evident to Brandon.

When we as leaders put aside our preoccupation with our value, it opens up a part of our brain that cares about the bigger picture. Empathizing instead of judging taps into our deep reservoirs of caring and belonging. We become committed to the "context" around us.

Think of context as the culture, environment, and underlying conditions in which we operate. The quality of our context is crucial because it significantly influences the choices we believe are possible. In an organizational context of distrust and competition, for example, it will feel risky to be authentic or collaborative. In a societal context of blame and demonizing others, most executives will think twice before publicly admitting a mistake. More broadly, the proving and defensive reactions of our egosystem invariably create contexts of stress, conflict, separation, close-mindedness, and making bad.

If we think about context at all, we tend to see it as external and somewhat static. But, like culture, the countless factors forging our context are almost entirely created by people. *As executives, each behavior we model and every decision we make contributes to the context inside and outside of our organizations.* When we are able to focus on what we truly want to create, we model a context of authenticity, learning, and connection. We stop perpetuating fear and start offering inspiration.

"These societal problems are both personal and collective," Peter Senge says. "Like droplets of water making tracks in the soil, they start with a few individuals. But the water that comes after follows those tracks until it becomes a river. Then not even the most heroic individual can change the direction by him- or herself.

"The danger of this thinking lies in concluding that there is nothing an individual can do," he continues. "Brandon's story is a beautiful example of how one person can influence the collective."

LaL cofounder Claire Nuer taught that "each of us has the possibility of being a rock that changes the course of the river." When we make good, our behavior allows others to be more aware of what type of river we're all forming—and every time we do it, it makes a difference. Brandon's empathy and vulnerability opened a quality of dialogue that allowed opposing groups to create an initial foundation of trust. He grasped the legitimacy of the nonprofits' point of view, and shared his own in a way that allowed them to see Encore's employees as well-intended, imperfect humans vs. agents of evil. Wanting the nonprofits to see Encore differently began with Brandon *behaving* differently.

Brandon found this clarity and courage through caring about the context Encore was creating. He was hoping his commitment would build a bridge with the coalition of nonprofits. He didn't suspect that his holistic mindset would give him and his team insight and inspiration that would electrify their workforce and differentiate their company.

BRANDON

Upon our return from New York, I charged a task force with examining our operations to identify any other unintended consequences like those the coalition had raised and to recommend changes that could make our processes more consumer-friendly. Greg Call, our associate general counsel, and Ashish led it. In mid-August, Paul and I met with them to review their conclusions.

Their most important recommendation focused on addressing the fear, confusion, and distrust consumers felt toward the collections process. They wanted to clearly lay out people's options in a Consumer Bill of Rights. They believed we could change the dialogue between consumers and debt collectors by publicly declaring our intentions and commitments. I had been expecting suggestions for operational changes and maybe a consumer help page on our website. I loved how ambitious their vision was.

Once it was clear Paul and I bought in, they urged me to consider making this an industry-wide effort. They believed a broad, inclusive vision could begin to change the spirit of discussions with the legislative and regulatory entities examining our industry.

I thought a Consumer Bill of Rights would resonate with Jim and the nonprofit coalition, but I was hesitant to expand the universe of participants. The proposed changes were well above and beyond what was required by the law. Encore was finally going to be viewed in a favorable light and—I hoped—I was going to be the subject of a positive news article. Why would we let other people in the industry get the benefit of our initiative?

"Because this isn't about you or Encore," said Greg. "This is about establishing a new paradigm for collections. We can't do that alone!"

He was right. Greg, Ashish, and the task force would begin drafting the principles of the Consumer Bill of Rights while I tried to schedule a meeting with our remaining competitors.

I couldn't remember a time when the leaders of our industry got together for a beer, let alone to tackle an important topic. If it happened, I wasn't invited. I realized my deeper reluctance to contact my peers came from the worry they wouldn't be interested. I'd look weak and inept to my team if everybody blew me off. But I could hear Shayne's voice: "So what if they reject you? Is that more important than improving the industry?"

I made the calls, suggesting an upcoming conference as a venue to meet. To my surprise, they all flew out a day early to talk about an industry-wide Consumer Bill of Rights. We were all worried about the looming regulatory pressure and wanted to get ahead of any reactive legislation. Unfortunately, when one company agreed with one of our proposals, another didn't, and vice versa. Despite hours of negotiating, we couldn't align on a single basic change—much less some of the more radical ideas that Encore wanted to pursue.

Greg looked over at me mid-afternoon. "We're wasting our time here," he said. I nodded in agreement.

We had more success with the nonprofit groups. They reviewed our proposals and suggested edits. We couldn't resolve all our disagreements, but both teams worked diligently. I was amazed that only a few months prior our entire relationship consisted of unproductive shouting matches. Now I was grateful for how they engaged with us: Their contributions were key. By December, we had almost finalized the document. Our last major hurdle was related to stopping some long-standing industry practices.

"There are three items in the Consumer Bill of Rights that could negatively impact revenues," I recapped for Paul and Greg in a final review meeting. "No longer reselling consumer accounts to other collection companies; eliminating all fees and interest for people on payment plans; and granting permanent relief from future collection efforts for people who are unlikely to ever recover financially."

"Were our statistical analysts able to quantify the financial impact?" asked Paul.

"No," I responded. "They've tried to simulate consumer behavior after the changes, but there are too many assumptions to create anything accurate. We could lose money, break even—there's even a chance we'll collect more. It depends on what you believe."

"The fact that no one else in the industry wanted to join us does give me pause," said Greg. "This is a one-way street, you know. Once we make these changes, there's no going back. We would get hammered by the press."

"Does that mean you're against it?" I asked.

"No, just the opposite. I want us to take a stand and set the standard for the industry. But we can't view these commitments as temporary. For us to gain people's trust, we need to stick to our word."

I felt torn. I wanted to change the collections process for consumers, but I also had a responsibility to the business. What if this backfired?

"One of the big things we learned last summer was that our customers don't understand or trust the collections process," Paul summarized. "When they keep getting charged interest, they feel like they can never pay it off. So they avoid the whole system."

"We all lose," Greg agreed. "They don't get out of debt, and we spend even more money trying to track them down."

"So we change the paradigm and deal with them straight up," I said, finishing up the logic we were talking ourselves through. "No hidden tricks. We act on the belief that if we're caring and trustworthy, they'll deal with us first. We also give them the comfort that they will only ever have to work with us. We won't resell their debt, and they won't have to tell their story over and over again to other companies. More people, more quickly, move out of debt. Our collections are at least as good, and our account managers feel better about their work."

"As a person, I want to make these changes," Paul said. "But as CFO, I'm worried. We do larger deals with more preferential pricing than most of our competitors. That gives us the ability to turn around and sell some accounts for a profit. Giving that up could be a big deal."

We were silent for a few seconds, and then Greg said, "We're taking the chance that consumer trust is worth more."

The three of us looked at each other, and nodded.

Our plan was to announce the Consumer Bill of Rights shortly after our earnings release in February 2011. We reached out to the nonprofit coalition one more time, wanting to put out a joint press release.

"You have to understand," Jim said. "We're uncomfortable endorsing anything that suggests alignment with or sympathy toward your company. You can mention our contribution, but please don't use our name."

I understood their concerns, but felt let down. We were missing an opportunity to demonstrate that it was possible to bridge breakdowns between companies and stakeholders.

In total, the Consumer Bill of Rights laid out thirty-six core principles that our consumers could expect from Encore. We didn't just agree to comply with the law; we agreed to be held to a higher moral and ethical standard.

CHAPTER 9

TELL ME AGAIN, WHAT GETS YOU UP IN THE MORNING?

The Inspiration of a Noble Goal

BRANDON

Encore India had a fantastic year in 2010. To my surprise, however, our success was met with outright skepticism. Many analysts, lenders, and investment bankers found our performance too impressive to believe. When they spoke to companies in the industry, our results were mocked with incredulity. Most, if not all, of our competitors had tried similar strategies and failed miserably. What could Encore be doing that was so unique? People seemed to think we were succeeding through some kind of sleight of hand.

We needed to demonstrate India's contribution in a different way, so we leveraged the adage "A picture is worth a thousand words." We invited our key constituents to participate in a two-day meeting in India in late January 2011 designed to showcase our world-class management team, employees, and facility.

Even in 2011, many Americans still had the impression that agents calling from India had thick accents and limited education. Our reality was totally different. Virtually all of our call center agents had begun learning English from a young age and had a college education. They could communicate just as effectively as our agents in the United States. The collection results spoke volumes.

ENCORE INDIA COLLECTION REVENUE (2007–2010)

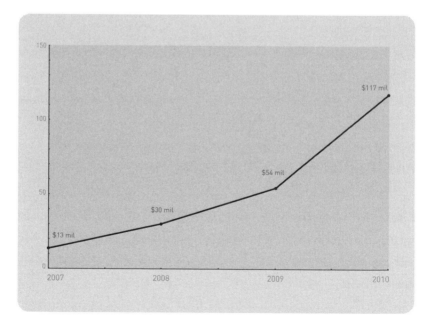

After some introductory comments from Manu, we let our guests wander around the call center floor for hours and gave them the flexibility to sit next to anybody they wanted to. No chaperones and no handpicked account managers. I was incredibly proud of what Manu and his team had accomplished, and what we had created together. I was betting our hard work would speak for itself.

When our guests got back to the conference room, they were astounded by the professionalism and competence. They compared notes and shared stories about the people they met. It was an amazing moment of vindication, particularly for Paul and me. We had faced so much doubt and resistance—India had seemed doomed to fail so many times—and now, they had surpassed our wildest expectations.

Our guests were particularly interested in our "One Team, One Dream" initiative, which kept coming up in their meetings. Manu hadn't addressed the initiative in his opening remarks, so I took a few moments to describe how the initiative came about.

I explained that Encore employees contacted consumers from our call centers: St. Cloud, Minnesota; San Diego; Phoenix; and New Delhi, India. We had hired more than six hundred new collectors in the previous eighteen months, mostly in India. Although excited about the growth and seemingly secure in their own jobs, the US workforces were still somewhat dismayed by the growing contribution coming from India. Tensions were down, but each center still operated as an island.

"One Team, One Dream" changed all that. This wasn't a corporate initiative—I didn't even know about it until after it launched. It was a grassroots movement started by lower-level call center managers from the United States and India who wanted to connect our employees around the globe. Each operating site designated a champion, and these individuals traveled to the other sites and worked alongside local employees. Instead of seeing each other as faceless people halfway around the world, they wanted to bring out the human side of the workforce. These "visitors" were embraced as real people, and likewise gained an appreciation for their colleagues and the different cultures that they were exposed to during their travels. They shared stories, customs, and holidays. Indian employees celebrated the Fourth of July, and U.S. employees celebrated Diwali, the Hindu festival of lights. It was truly inspiring how many people had put aside their beliefs and fears to create a cohesive multicultural unit.

One Team, One Dream had been fundamental to our success. The connection and mutual respect built between the different sites had become the foundation that allowed us to add new work departments in India. Besides the 1,500 collection agents within the four call centers, we now had hundreds of information technology personnel, analysts, and administrative staff. These new groups were performing critical tasks and providing us with an unprecedented ability to scale across our business.

Many analyst reports documented their experience. Their validation of our strategy finally put to rest any remaining doubts about our success in India.

I had one other significant moment during that trip. The flight home from New Delhi to San Diego takes about twenty-four hours from takeoff to touchdown. I often passed the time watching videos, playing games, or reading something inspirational. This time, however, I couldn't concentrate on reading, and I turned my attention instead to a few TED talks I had downloaded. One of them was Simon Sinek's video, "How Great Leaders Inspire Action."

One thing he was especially passionate about caught my attention: "It's not *what* you do that matters. It's *why* you do it."

It got me thinking. Why did we do this work at Encore? For the shareholders? To preserve the banking system?

Those were true, but consumers caught in a web of debt didn't care about shareholder profits. They were just trying to survive. Our

Consumer Bill of Rights was a step toward identifying the why—the "inner circle" in Sinek's video. But it still didn't capture our essential purpose. What, really, were we offering our customers? What was the essential motivation at the core of our actions?

Back at headquarters, we started having discussions as an executive team and from these we developed and circulated a series of statements. My favorite was "restoring dignity and creating a path toward financial independence." Our account managers often spoke about how our customers felt trapped by past decisions and were looking for a way out. People in debt didn't feel good about themselves, and the constant collection calls only reminded them that they hadn't lived up to their promises.

Although not yet fully articulated, this *essential why* began shaping how we interacted with our consumers and the very way we thought about our work.

SHAYNE

"People at Encore were jazzed by the Consumer Bill of Rights," Brandon recalled. "It gave them a sense of pride about our company. I never saw that level of enthusiasm for quarterly results or a new strategy."

As Brandon and the team began humanizing their consumers, it expanded their ability to build authentic relationships with them. Instead of trying to extract money from debtors—which made Encore employees see others as obstacles to overcome and put them at the mercy—they focused on working with people in financial difficulty to help them get back on their feet. By making this shift they empathized with debtors and supported them. Instead of feeling righteous, ambivalent, or numb, many workers at Encore began to feel enthusiastic and at the source about their work.

Their experience highlights a simple truth: Each of us has *a powerful need to positively affect the people and world around us.* This need and inspiration is what we call our "noble goal."

In its simplest form, our noble goal is our personal response to the question "What context, atmosphere, or environment do I want to create for myself and others?" In the narrow, scarcity mindset of our egosystem, we lose our care for others and the broader perspective. We create environments of distrust, competition, animosity, and separation. But when we are connected to our noble goal, its clarity inspires us and guides us toward what we really care to bring about in the world, in all domains of our life—our families, our workplaces, our communities, and our society. It is our North Star, and it has the power to guide both our long-term direction as well as our moment-by-moment choices.

Even if we haven't yet put our noble goal into words, we all have this yearning inside us. If we look at our life, we can see it showing up in our actions. Brandon's noble goal, for example, was to "see every person as a human being in need of something." This guided his decision to dialogue with the nonprofit groups who were critical of him. It was the instinct that led him to empathize with his consumers.

When Amy took on the diversity challenge at Encore, it was as much for other women as for herself. Encore's executive team supported the effort because they wanted to create a fair work environment. They just needed Amy's courage to see that it was missing.

This desire to elevate those around us is in our DNA, and the energy we feel when we act on this instinct elevates our focus, enthusiasm, and creativity to a new level. It gives us the courage to take risks we might not otherwise dare to. When Jim Syran walked the floor at the Phoenix call center during the layoff in 2007, he felt inspired to show up for others in a way that terrified him. Prioritizing our caring and empathy over our personal discomfort is characteristic of our noble goal. It helps us behave in ways that encompass the needs of everybody involved.

An organization can have a noble goal too. This is frequently clearer for nonprofits or socially responsible businesses, whose mission is explicitly outward focused. Yet Encore's example helps break a false duality when we talk about purpose: that what our company does is either inherently selfish or altruistic.

When Brandon and his team created the Consumer Bill of Rights, it felt scary and risky to break the mold. But ultimately, they felt more inspired, and it empowered employees to act from this space of caring. Every interaction became an opportunity to create a context of trust and honesty. Morale increased and collections continued to grow.

This more empathic approach inspired Encore's VP of Marketing, Brian Enneking, to develop Encore Capital's Consumer Yearbook, which chronicled their interactions with consumers. "I felt compelled to start the initiative even though it wasn't one of my objectives," Brian explained. "Executive leadership was encouraging us to think and care about the consumer, and they *meant* it. People believed it."

"I am relieved to have something worked out on my account," writes one consumer. "I truly appreciate [your] help in resolving my debt," says another. Page after page of feedback reflects the appreciation and relief people experienced in interacting with Encore's collectors. They were scared, confused, and needed help. When a collector phoned, many consumers began to see the person as their ally in navigating the system.

It wasn't just that these account managers had strong customer service skills. Something else guided their behavior. Interviews with them show that Encore's focus on *having an intention for their consumers* spoke to employees. "It gives me a sense of pride and honor knowing that I am able to improve someone's financial situation," states a young collector in Encore's India call center. Another talks about reminding himself that "each consumer has his or her own personal story or journey that got them into this financial situation. It is my job to listen, ask questions, and then offer solutions. When I hear their gratitude, it puts a spring in my step and more energy in my voice."

Every job, no matter the profession, serves a deep purpose—but we may need to look for it beyond the blinders of our egosystem. If a debt collection company can feel genuinely inspired by a noble goal, it is accessible to all of us.

The Power of Commitment in the Face of Failure

BRANDON

One critically important item needed to be finalized before our earnings release in February 2011. After the affidavit ruling back in 2009, at least ten plaintiffs' attorneys from separate jurisdictions across the country filed lawsuits to have our judgments overturned or vacated. It would have been a nightmare to deal with all of them individually, so we had the cases consolidated into a national class action in the state of Ohio. After eighteen months of negotiation, we had reached an agreement that resolved all matters.

During these negotiations, we established that although we had made a critical misstep in the wording of our paperwork, the consumers in question did in fact owe the money. Nonetheless, to avoid a lengthy and costly legal battle, we agreed to pay over $5 million to settle the matter. We believed this was more than fair, given the lack of economic impact to any of the consumers involved. All parties agreed, and the federal judge gave his preliminary approval to the settlement several days later.

Everything was lined up for the announcement of our financial results for 2010. Collections had increased 25 percent, while our cost-to-collect declined by 10 percent and our cash flow and earnings grew by 30 percent. In addition, we had raised another $75 million in capital to acquire new portfolios. Our shareholders were pleased, and Encore's stock ended February around $27 per share—almost ten times higher than the low point in April 2009!

It's fun to be the CEO of a public company when the stock is going up. Existing shareholders congratulate you on your results; prospective shareholders take your calls and are keenly interested in your story; the employees love coming to work. We had been on an amazing run since mid-2009, and I saw nothing but clear skies ahead.

Almost on cue, lightning struck. Within days of the class action settlement, outright anger was expressed in many newspapers, including the *Wall Street Journal*, about the perceived unfairness of the terms. Pleas were made to state officials to stand up for their constituents. We were in the spotlight, and it was white hot.

After making some calls, we determined that much of the outrage was fueled by misinformation. Behind closed doors, we were being accused of everything from filing fake lawsuits against people who didn't owe any money to blatantly disregarding the laws in individual states. Every day, it seemed another state or group came out against the settlement.

The allegations hurt. I felt judged as unethical, and it struck a deep nerve. Didn't it matter that a federal judge and a team of plaintiffs' attorneys had spent two years reviewing extensive amounts of information before agreeing to the settlement? Who were these people to question our integrity without ever meeting with me or with anyone on my team? I felt out of control and desperately wanted to set the record straight.

Initially, we managed the public relations backlash pretty well. Several newspaper articles fanned the flames, but they were largely based on hearsay and rhetoric. We kept restating the facts, which were well founded and seemed indisputable. I tried to reassure the employees and our shareholders that it was a tempest in a teapot. Once the various state officials fully understood the due diligence that went into the settlement, they would move on to something else. The judge signed the formal agreement on March 9, which helped bolster our position. We continued working with the states, and our shareholders seemed satisfied with our answers.

The negative reaction to the settlement prompted us to delay our announcement of the Consumer Bill of Rights. We didn't want it to be seen as deflecting attention from the lawsuit, but we didn't want to lose momentum on it either. On March 21, when we finally presented it publicly, our employees were enthusiastic and proud to be leading the modernization of the collection industry.

The excitement lasted exactly one week. On March 28, the attorney general of Minnesota sued us for a variety of offenses, including systematically collecting from the wrong people. They hadn't spoken with us beforehand, and I couldn't figure out what information they were using upon which to base their claims. Everything seemed to be coming from third parties. We contacted the attorney general's office, hoping that things could be resolved quickly.

In the meantime, I continued to believe that Encore could get a fair hearing in the media. Encouraged by our relationship with the consumer groups, I thought if I had honest and vulnerable conversations with journalists, maybe I could break through the mutual distrust we had with the press. I explained the facts as we saw them to one journalist covering our industry, sharing in our phone conversation how we were just people trying to fulfill our duty in a productive way. I answered her questions transparently and hung up feeling that we had built an understanding. When the article came out, however, it was as if we'd never spoken. The press about Encore and the lawsuit remained one-sided and, at times, very personal.

The saddest part for me was the assertion that we had opportunistically issued the Consumer Bill of Rights. No matter what we did, the world was always going to see us as the bad guys. I was starting to feel numb and cynical again.

Then in July, the state of Texas sued us for items related to the affidavit issue. It just wouldn't end. The press jumped all over it. Other states threatened to start an investigation into our collection practices. The court of public opinion was hanging us.

When I went into our executive staff meeting the following week, I found that my whole team, like me, was frustrated and discouraged. Instead of talking about financial results, ongoing initiatives, or portfolio opportunities, we quizzed Greg Call, now our general counsel, desperate for some kind of resolution. We were theorizing about what would happen if this dragged on much longer when Manu cut us off.

"Why are we spending so much time talking about this?" he asked over the videoconference from India.

"I'm getting questions from the banks about the status of these lawsuits," Amy told him. "If we don't fix this, they'll stop selling accounts to us."

"And our shareholders don't know what to believe," added Paul. "Our stock is getting killed."

"I understand," Manu countered, "but I also know that we consistently make ethical decisions about how we collect. We spent *thousands* of man-hours implementing processes to live up to our Consumer Bill of Rights. My collectors here are excited to help people get back on track. We need to have faith in Greg and his team to manage these lawsuits. We can't control what the media says about us," he exclaimed, "but we can trust ourselves and focus on our work!"

Manu was right. I felt my energy shifting back to what mattered. Seeing people around the table soak in his words, I felt embarrassed that

I wasn't the one to put us back on track. But that was why I built this supportive team, and let go of being the smartest person in the room. It didn't matter who brought the clarity, it mattered that we found it.

In the coming weeks, we stopped defending ourselves; instead, we thought about how to get the facts transparently on the table. No one wanted to believe we had made structural changes to our processes or that we were not intentionally trying to harm consumers. Just as stock analysts had validated our success in India, we needed somebody from outside Encore to authenticate what we were doing. The Texas attorney general's office became that entity.

We were openly challenged and audited by them between July and December 2011. During that time, our stock price once again dropped by a material amount, from $30 per share to $20. I can't claim that I was never demoralized by the ups and downs, but our team did an amazing job of sticking together and supporting each other. In the end, no consequential issues were uncovered, and our investors, analysts, and key bank clients began to accept our facts as true. The storm clouds were clearing.

Many other states were still unconvinced. Realizing that openness was our best path, we discussed asking those groups to form a coalition to audit us. It seemed crazy. If we let them poke around, who knew what they might find? Conceivably, there were issues I didn't know about or inadvertent inefficiencies that looked bad.

But the team and I ultimately decided we were confident in our operations. And if they found something, it would help us improve.

We put out the invitation, and the states in question agreed to identify representatives to examine our operations and processes. It would take time, but we'd work together to make it all-encompassing and completely transparent. At last, we had a path to closure.

Throughout dealing with all these legal issues, we never finalized the articulation of our noble goal. The absence of a definitive version didn't diminish how important our consumer-centric approach had become for us, however.

SHAYNE

A debt collection company like Encore Capital—with the Wall Street pressure for quarterly results and the uncomfortable task of collecting money from reluctant consumers—is an extreme example of a chronic experience in the modern world. Leaders and employees in all sectors—public, private, nonprofit—are often too stressed to feel inspired. Even organizations with an inspiring mission can get caught up in the grind. *What makes it so difficult to live a life infused by our noble goal?*

Feeling a daily connection to a larger calling occurs when our brain is predominantly preoccupied by our sense of purpose. Many of us in the Western world, however, focus on our personal success as the yardstick of our value. The drive to achieve and the fear of failure dominate our thinking. Year after year, we work long hours, pushing ourselves to ever-higher heights—the next promotion, recognition, or financial threshold—only to discover that the high of accomplishment disappears in minutes or days. Slight underperformance triggers our egosystem's fear of not being good enough. This quasi-permanent stress squashes the inspiration of our noble goal.

This is the "*performance anxiety paradigm*" in which our yearning for success and our fear of failure become our primary obsession. Although many leaders credit their fear of failure for driving them to succeed, inherently it is an at the mercy mindset. We are driven, believing (falsely) that we will feel "good enough" when we've reached whatever success milestone we are chasing after. But we won't. Have you noticed how quickly the feeling of inadequacy returns? No amount of external success will satiate our egosystem's potent mixture of anxiety and delusions of grandeur. Our path as leaders is to let go of this hopeless hope and be guided instead by what we want to create and contribute with others.

Having this performance anxiety paradigm as our dominant frame of reference isn't "bad," but it does have consequences. For starters, performance anxiety infuses us with a sense of scarcity in time, achievement, money, and reputation. We can never do enough, the result being that we often de-prioritize other aspects of our life, such as family, physical and mental well-being, and involvement in our community. Similarly, it can undermine the quality and integrity of our professional endeavors. Our zero-sum mindset about success, profitability, and performance can push us to make "me first" or even ethically gray decisions. If criticisms later arise, we're often defensive because we sense we've compromised ourselves.

Root-cause analyses of British Petroleum's Deepwater Horizon explosion on the Gulf Coast in 2010 revealed that cost-cutting and overly aggressive schedules fostered a culture of poor safety. It was easy to demonize BP and the workforce that allowed this disaster to happen, but frankly, *most organizations in every industry function similarly*. As a society, we have created a context where financial results and the performance anxiety paradigm, not purpose or contribution to society, reign supreme. Think this tendency is "out there"? Just notice how you feel the next time a colleague or a competitor is advancing faster than you are. Chances are you will feel a twinge—a pinch—and feel compelled to race ahead. It's a collective obsession that has consequences for all of us.

Although Encore Capital never finalized their company's noble goal, their story illustrates the power of *searching* for it. Leadership sincerely cared about their consumers and employees, and that created a context of purpose in the organization. Empathy influenced employee decisions and behaviors when no one was watching. Later, when Encore was under fire, they had nothing to hide in how they operated. It didn't mean they were perfect, but Brandon and the team felt secure enough to say to their detractors, *Come take a look and tell us what you find.*

Their noble goal helped rouse this courage because failing, being judged, and feeling hurt seemed less threatening. If there were flaws in their system, they *wanted* to learn about them because it accelerated their ability to fulfill their mission. Our noble goal helps us better see others' needs and be more willing to learn when our ego feels incompetent. It is a central ingredient in any learning organization.

This freedom causes us to show up more often with our full talents and strengths. Our mental faculties focus on what really matters and how to do it to the utmost of our abilities. We create positive ripple effects, because we're more willing to see others succeed and even outshine us. We grow, we collaborate, and we give discretionary effort. A meaningful noble goal inspires significantly higher performance long term for individuals and organizations.

Uncomfortably, the freedom and creativity of being at the source comes when we let go of the results that feel most imperative to achieve. Letting go of the result does not mean letting go of our commitment to our goals, but rather accepting that we might not achieve the outcomes our ego so craves.

We saw this in Manu's intervention in Brandon's executive staff meeting. It would be easy to think now that Encore could afford to be at the source because they had achieved their business results. But far more often, it seemed they would never get there. Their stock was down. The media was castigating them. "There were many times I felt we were failing," Brandon recalled.

That is the anxious chatter of our ego. We always have the choice, in the context of our noble goal, to say "so what?" We might fail. We might be judged, or hurt, or not get that promotion we're so desiring.

But what do we want? How do we want to grow? What context do we want to create?

In the words of Claire Nuer, "When we say 'so what?' to our deepest fears and reach for the stars, the magic of being human unfolds."

To truly become a different type of collection company—a model for the industry to emulate—we needed more than just the Consumer Bill of Rights. The executive team and I spent many hours searching for initiatives that could bring benefits to our current and future customers.

My favorite idea involved forgiving $1 billion in debt. Now *that* would be a good headline! How could releasing 500,000 people from at least one of their debt obligations be spun negatively? Our analytics were accurate enough to assure that doing this would not impact Encore's bottom line, and it would move hundreds of thousands of people closer to financial solvency.

Everybody loved the idea—until we focused on an unintended consequence for our consumers. The federal tax code has a provision that requires any forgiven debt of more than a few hundred dollars to be reported to the Internal Revenue Service as income. Given that the average balance was around $2,000 for the identified accounts, we could actually harm our consumers' tax status by canceling their obligation. As crazy as it sounded, our customers were better off if we did nothing and maintained the obligations as "outstanding."

The idea I became most excited about involved bringing together a group of prominent researchers, nonprofit organizations, and our own internal team of behavioral scientists to study how our consumers make financial decisions.

Even though our consumers accounted for 10 to 20 percent of the U.S. population, there were virtually no systematic efforts to understand them. There were many anecdotes but only limited data. Doing research of any kind required access to a large database of consumers, and we happened to have one of the largest databases of financially distressed consumers in the country. Understanding our consumers better would allow for better communication, a higher level of engagement, and likely better financial returns with fewer complaints. More broadly, this knowledge would enable us to bring data to the growing number of discussions about what to do for overstretched consumers. It would be good for us, good for the consumer, and good for the system. The Consumer Financial Protection Bureau had announced its intention to hold field meetings to discuss what was "wrong" with collections. This initiative could allow us to move beyond the anecdotes we expected would dominate the discussions.

From the outset, I struggled with the notion of Encore funding something like this. Who would believe we were trying to better understand our consumers for reasons other than making more money? Given our previous experience with nonprofits, would any important groups be willing to openly partner with us? Was such a public benefit initiative the right kind of investment for a for-profit company to make?

I decided if we were serious about understanding our consumers and committed to being a constructive voice in the discussion about the collection industry, it was an imperative. We discussed the idea with our board and they were supportive of us moving forward. The benefits of bringing together a broad coalition of partners to develop data and analyses that could shift the dialogue toward facts instead of emotions and anecdotes far outweighed the monetary cost and the potential of being second-guessed about our motives. We funded the Consumer Credit Research Institute and announced it publicly in December 2011. Our partners included some of the leading universities in the country, nonprofit groups, and the Urban Institute.

CHAPTER 10

WHY IT ALL MATTERS

Working on Your Ego Is the Highest Act of Leadership

BRANDON

From 2009 to 2011, our cash flows, revenues, and earnings increased at a compounded rate of 25 percent. Our analysts and investors expected that to continue into the future, of course. Due to the slowdown in lending after the financial crisis of 2008–2009, however, banks now had 50 percent less distressed debt. This created a dearth of new portfolio opportunities, leading to our industry's second dramatic price increase in the previous seven years. Fortunately, India was saving us tens of millions of dollars a year in operating expenses, which gave us much greater purchasing flexibility. Even so, the embedded growth expectations seemed barely feasible.

In February 2012, we assembled our global leadership team for a two-day strategic planning retreat. We met shortly after the launching of our new call center in Costa Rica, designed to service those customers whose preferred language was Spanish. Our first order of business was to talk about the implications of the Consumer Financial Protection Bureau's decision to directly oversee our industry. The bureau's charter was to protect American consumers who were in the market for financial products and services. This meant everything from loan origination to collections. The bureau had published a 950-page compliance and examination manual in October 2011 and could show up on our doorstep any time after January 1, 2013. Encore had never been under the direct oversight of a regulatory body and getting ready for our first audit would be a monumental undertaking.

Besides preparing for the bureau's audit and expanding our Costa Rica site, three potential strategic priorities competed for our attention: acquire a new company, purchase a sizable portfolio, and divest ourselves of a struggling acquisition. All were intriguing, and each presented its own set of challenges.

Our biggest opportunity—and my team's greatest concern—was the acquisition of a company outside of our core competence. Our track record on acquisitions was zero for one, so I wanted everybody's thoughts on whether this one could be different. We discussed the takeaways from our 2005 acquisition, including how I failed to outline clear expectations and hold the management team accountable. We concluded that the current opportunity had significantly more promise. There was a strong cultural fit with the leadership team, their business would leverage our core capabilities, and it was large enough to meaningfully impact Encore's bottom line. Everybody was excited and hopeful we could complete the negotiation.

This wasn't enough to hit our growth target, however. In addition,

Amy was proposing to purchase the legacy portfolio of one of our largest competitors, who had stopped acquiring new portfolios in 2011. This $150 million transaction would be the largest in Encore's history. Besides the large price tag, we would need to stage the introduction of the accounts into our system to avoid overwhelming our employees and undercutting the performance of other portfolios. Although it would be the most operationally complex deal we ever completed, there was little debate. We had previously completed several transactions with failing competitors and had learned how to integrate them.

Our last potential initiative was a long time coming. Our 2005 acquisition had barely been profitable for us and hadn't added a meaningful client in two years. It was time to move on—but how could we do so without negatively impacting the workforce?

Reflecting during a break, I had a feeling of déjà vu. It was 2005 all over again: In a very short time period, we would be attempting to simultaneously execute five complicated strategic initiatives. The results last time hadn't been pretty, and I didn't want to repeat the same mistake. I needed to limit our focus.

When we resumed, I told the leadership team, "I'm concerned that we're over-extending ourselves. Besides scaling up our site in Costa Rica and getting ready for the CFPB, we need to choose only one or two other initiatives."

"I'm confused," Paul asked. "Why would we limit ourselves?"

"Do you remember the last time we tried to take on too many things at once?" I asked.

"Only too well. But we're a tighter, deeper, and stronger team now. People think enterprise wide. We shift resources without drama when top priorities change. We solve challenges together instead of finger-pointing. Look at how we managed through the last two years. That should make all the difference."

I went around the room and, to my surprise, even the most conservative members of the management team agreed we could pursue all of these strategies *while* maintaining strong performance in our core business. I thought back to the Investment Committee meetings where I had so often pushed my team to be more aggressive. Now, I wasn't convincing them; they were convincing me! Despite the ups and downs of the past few years, this amazing group of people had maintained their resolve and positioned Encore to leap forward in the next few years. I was in awe of what we had become.

The element of the strategy I was directly responsible for was finding a suitable outcome for our legacy 2005 acquisition and its 150 employees. I was steadfast in my commitment to not cause people to unnecessarily lose their jobs. Just because I couldn't make the company work didn't mean it couldn't be successful. It was a long shot, but I believed it could be a good strategic fit for one particular company in our industry. I reached out to that company's CEO, and he did his due diligence. In the end, *we paid his company* $4.3 million to complete the sale. While unorthodox, the amount was identical to the cost we had projected to shut it down. It allowed the vast majority of our employees to retain their jobs.

The other transactions were proceeding forward, and we seemed likely to close all three deals around the same time, depending on the financing. Within a month, Paul and his team had raised the $275 million we needed, and the burden shifted to Greg and his Legal team. They worked tirelessly to simultaneously create new financing agreements along with three purchase and sale documents. Before leaving each day, I walked around the thirteenth floor of our headquarters in San Diego to check on morale. All the work we had done to build the team was being put to the test. Despite fatigue and eighteen-hour days, attitudes were upbeat.

Finance and Legal teams rarely get the credit they deserve, and I was never more appreciative of their efforts. On May 9, 2012, we announced the completion of all three transactions—as well as the result that collections, revenue, and earnings had increased by 20 percent in the first quarter! Everything had come together, just as my team had promised.

At our annual shareholder meeting in New York in June, I asked Manu to have lunch. I hadn't seen him in months, but when we sat down at the table, he reached into his briefcase and handed me an envelope. My heart dropped, fearing a resignation note. We were on such a roll.

I didn't want to open it, but when I looked up at the big grin on his face, I knew it must be something else. I would never have guessed in a thousand tries. A letter addressed to Manu from the Great Places to Work Institute had informed him that Encore India had been selected as thirty-seventh on the list of the "Best Companies to Work for in India"—two places above Johnson and Johnson and seven above Microsoft India. I didn't even know they had applied!

I was awestruck at the magnitude of this award. A start-up debt collection firm, struggling to survive as recently as 2007, was now one of the elite companies in all of India. A leadership team that was relentless about its own personal and team development had partnered with a workforce that cared about collective, not individual success. They had encouraged our U.S. team to challenge conventional wisdom and worked tirelessly to help people on the other side of the world get back on track financially. They didn't see themselves as a low-cost call center for an American company. They had proudly created an Indian company with its own brand and identity, and had sought to hire the best and brightest. They just happened to be in debt collections.

Two years later, they would rise to fourteenth on the list.

For the remainder of 2012, we focused on executing our plan and hitting our financial milestones. All five of our strategic initiatives were going as planned and our results increased each quarter. Our stock price increased 50 percent during the year, ending at $30 per share.

On the home front, Dana was in the second year of her Master's in Nonprofit Leadership program, Trevor was beginning high school, and Aidan and Leah were thriving in their Montessori school. Adding that to the successes at Encore, I felt truly blessed—but also somewhat guilty. Why were we so lucky? I began wondering if I had the right balance between work, family, and community.

This uneasy feeling was reinforced by the exposure Dana's program was giving me to leaders of nonprofit organizations in San Diego. These were immensely passionate individuals dedicating their lives to helping those less fortunate. I had always focused on work and spent little time giving back to the community. I wrote plenty of checks, but rarely gave any time. I was glad Dana was doing her part to represent our family, but still . . .

For the first time in my fifteen years, I thought about leaving Encore. Not in reaction to a fear of failure, like with Capital One, but from a place of curiosity about what could be next. I felt I would be leaving Encore in a stable place with a robust culture.

Dana and I talked at length, and she supported whatever decision I made. I spent time with friends and mentors to get their perspective and guidance. There were good reasons to make a change, but even stronger forces not to: stature, loyalty, and uncertainty. For almost a decade, much of my identity was tied to being the president and CEO of Encore. It came with a high level of access to money, people, and information. Most of my friends in San Diego held similar positions. Would they still accept me if I left Encore? What would I offer at social gatherings? I loved the people at Encore—would I be abandoning them? Were our relationships based solely on work? And what would I do if

I left? I hadn't gone two weeks without working since college. Could I succeed on my own?

I was scheduled to be a guest speaker at an upcoming LaL seminar. It was a short session in which participants take stock of their personal growth to date and work on any core beliefs holding them back. I was just supposed to share Encore's story of change, but I decided to redo the entire seminar to focus on these questions about leaving. I wanted to really look at my fears and find a way beyond them. Inertia is powerful. Even if I left Encore, I was afraid I'd take the comfortable route: get on a few boards, fall into whatever opportunities came my way. What did I really want to do? If I just ended up taking a CEO job elsewhere, why leave Encore?

Through the exercises and authentic conversations with other participants, I saw that all my questions were symptoms of unconscious fears and beliefs I had about my worth: "No matter how hard I work or what I do, I'll never be good enough." And "If I don't have a title, I don't matter." Stated out loud, they seemed silly—but I sensed these beliefs were holding me back from clarifying what I truly wanted.

After a lot of soul-searching, I decided I wanted to find a new path, one defined by conscious choices instead of riding along with the current. I regretted never coaching one of Trevor's sports teams, and I wanted a different outcome for Aidan and Leah. We had just four more years with Trevor before college and I wanted to make the most of them. I met with George Lund, who asked me to keep an open mind about staying. Meanwhile, the board evaluated options for finding a new CEO. I pushed forward with our initiatives.

In early April 2013, the board identified my successor and we announced my departure. I would stay on through a ninety-day transition period.

After the announcement, I was a little withdrawn, and I started moving on in my mind. Shayne must have sensed it when he was in town a few weeks later, because he started asking me what I felt.

"Not much" was my immediate answer.

"I think you're numbing, Brandon," he said to me directly. "In some ways, this has been your challenge from the beginning: You disconnect from others and how you're feeling.

"There are a lot of people who are grateful for their time with you," he continued. "They're going to be sad you're leaving. If you don't stay emotionally present till the end, you're not going to create the space for them to mourn this transition."

"Isn't that making it about me?" I asked. "I don't want to make a big deal of my departure."

"I'm talking about being real and authentic. You need that, and they need that."

Instead of rushing through to the end, I cherished each moment. I had meaningful discussions with one or two employees almost every day. Sometimes they just wanted to be reassured that nothing was wrong. Other times they wanted to share their favorite story or interaction.

A few weeks later, I toured our operating sites one last time to say goodbye and introduce the new CEO. An account manager pulled me aside in Phoenix.

"I'll always remember you as a simple person who left a profound impact on people," she said. "You always made me feel important. It was a true privilege to work with you."

I was about to brush it off, and then I stopped myself. As her words brought tears to my eyes, I let them fall. In fact, I let myself experience strong emotions many more times in the coming weeks as people shared their gratitude and memories with me. I hugged a bunch of people who meant the world to me.

At each site, I was given a book full of notes from employees. Almost nobody said what a visionary leader I was or how many smart decisions I made. Turns out people couldn't care less about my desired images of appearing smart and capable. Instead, they thanked me for little things like remembering their kids' names or walking around with my head up instead of looking down at my phone.

Mostly, they thanked me for treating them like human beings and for putting the right decision ahead of being right, and our collective goals ahead of looking good. People seemed to deeply trust that I would do what was best for the whole. Even more, that I encouraged them to act that way with each other and with our consumers. The note that inspired me the most came from Greg Call.

"I could write about your rare combination of sharp intellect and the ability to connect with people. But what impressed me the most over the years are the little things: making sure that everyone feels included, respected, and attended to. Thanks for the example you set."

Their words struck a chord in me. I competed for so long to be the smartest person in the room, to be the one in the spotlight. I thought that was how you led people—how you got recognition and success. If not for the work I did to challenge the self-worth drivers I didn't even know I had, I would probably still be that way.

I thought back to that day in 2007 when we had to terminate 10 percent of our workforce. I had felt nauseated and sworn I would never again let my ego prevent me from doing what was best for Encore. Looking back, I hadn't been perfect—but I had been *committed*.

I had listened, looked within, and developed a new way to lead. I learned to value transparency, empathy, and vulnerability as much as business intellect. Today, I'm able to be present with my colleagues, family, and friends; see different possibilities; and create a collective agenda instead of one dominated by my opinions. I believe Encore's runaway success was directly tied to this shift in management philosophy and culture. I just wish I had learned this lesson way back when I started leading people!

I was saying goodbye to Jessica, Brandon's executive assistant, after a day of consulting with him in 2012, when she pulled me aside.

"I wanted to thank you," she said. "I've never worked in a place like Encore. I felt it from day one, and it's only grown."

"What do you mean?" I asked.

"Life is simple here. Don't get me wrong, we work really hard—but all of my other jobs prior to this were . . . toxic. Gossiping, groups and people vying against each other, personal agendas. You never really knew whom you could trust. It was exhausting. I dreaded coming to the office. But here, there's genuine authenticity. I see it in the executive team, their direct reports, and it rubs off on all of us."

She touched her heart, seeming to refer to the cadre of executive assistants who supported the leadership team. "I really didn't think I wanted to come work for a debt collection company, but I love it here."

The emotion of her words stayed with me as I flew home, and I later shared it with the rest of the LaL team. As much as I get excited by helping organizations collaborate more effectively to achieve daunting challenges, moments like Jessica's words of gratitude reconnect me even more deeply with my noble goal of healing the pain and separation caused by our egos. Each of my colleagues has been inspired over the years by our clients' sense of relief and gratitude when they can really let down their guard and bring their whole selves to their work relationships.

The experience Jessica described goes to the heart of why Brandon and I wrote this book, and why LaL teaches this work. Too many organizations, families, and public arenas are infected by politics and performance anxiety pressure. But this chronic egosystem context is totally unnecessary.

When we create a culture of emotional safety in our teams and organizations, we allow people to deactivate these self-preservation behaviors. Relationships become simpler, initiatives more inspiring. We find the courage to acknowledge our shortcomings and work on them transparently. "How do I feel?!" one senior executive exclaimed recently to a colleague of mine. His incessant mind chatter had vanished. "I've got half of my brain back and I didn't even know it was missing." When leaders model and welcome self-awareness around ego drivers, they help unleash people's full potential. Our energy focuses on growing, being connected to others, and co-creating something larger.

Each of us brims with this incredible generosity and creativity. We are wholly capable of putting aside our ego's ambitions to reach with others for a higher calling. Not only do we not have to build our lives and careers at the expense of others—we don't *want* to.

In 2008, just a few months after Encore's significant layoff, Brandon held a town hall meeting in India. At the end, Vikram, one of their top account managers, pulled him aside.

"What do Encore employees in the U.S. think of India?" he asked Brandon.

Unsure of Vikram's intent, Brandon hesitated. Then he told him the truth. "They don't understand," he responded. "And mostly, they're afraid."

"Afraid of what?"

"Of losing their jobs."

"*We don't want to succeed at their expense,*" Vikram responded forcefully. He grabbed Brandon's arm and looked him right in the eye. "I want you to tell them that. Promise me you will!"

Brandon was moved by Vikram's passion and boldness. "Our Indian employees lived in far more challenging conditions than our U.S. workforce," Brandon told me later, "and yet *they* were concerned about *our* welfare. They wanted their success to buoy the United States, not undermine or replace."

People yearn for a different paradigm. When we make others good, we build a momentum of trust and inspiration. We think about contributing instead of winning. Each additional person who steps up creates positive ripples throughout an organization—and, the more senior you are, the more impactful your behavior.

At different points over the past few years, I doubted whether it was wise to write a book with the CEO of a debt collection company. Would LaL be judged for associating with this industry?

It was a risk—but it was outweighed by the opportunity to question our conviction, in all aspects of our lives, that there are heroes and villains. That colleague or department that doesn't get it? You now know to identify how it serves your egosystem to make them bad. That company or industry that is a menace to society? Sorry, but the people working in it are just like you and me. Struggling to get by or get ahead, feeling too stressed to be guided by a noble goal, or too powerless or righteous to consider the consequences of their actions inside or outside their organization. Not because they don't care, but because their egosystem, like yours and mine, is preoccupied by self-worth. Every time we react to an email, or vent about that other department, or judge silently in our mind, we perpetuate a context of egosystem behaviors. Every time we castigate people on the other side of an issue, we help ensure that the gridlock continues.

But an individual named Brandon, who just happened to be the CEO of a public company, had the courage to really question himself— time and time again. To appear imperfect or inferior; to accept that he might be wrong; to choose his goals for the larger context even when it felt vulnerable for his ego. It sounds so straightforward, yet perhaps you sense how rare it is. And within Encore, leader after leader took similar risks.

We each have this choice. At every moment, we either fuel or transcend these collective dysfunctions. While Brandon and Encore's transformation happened over a period of time, you as a leader have the ability to start showing up differently at work and at home *tomorrow*:

- Notice the moments in your life when you experience a pinch. It might be an event or something someone says or does.

- Instead of reacting, search for what is triggered in you. What is that visceral discomfort you're trying to numb or you're blaming others for? How is your sense of self-worth threatened?

- Look outward and consider what vulnerabilities others might be feeling behind their veneer of strength or indifference. Empathize with how they feel in danger.

- Take the risk of disclosing how you feel vulnerable. Share your ego threat, not your mind chatter. Model a context of safety.

If you want the politics and turf wars in your organization to stop, it starts with you. Working on yourself is the highest act of leadership.

Brandon and I are counting on you. In the end, this book isn't just about your development as a leader or the performance of your organization. It's about what we're capable of creating together when we break out of the prison of our ego.

ACKNOWLEDGMENTS

Significant Contribution

We want to express our gratitude to Noah Nuer for your commitment and contributions to this book. From crafting the narrative to clarifying key ideas to helping with the book's design, you have been an instrumental contributor. Without your pushback and suggestions, this book would not be where it is today.

Brandon Black

To my best friend and partner in life, Dana. Without you, the Encore journey ends very differently, and this book never gets written. Thank you for insisting that I always strive to be a better father and husband.

To my parents, for pushing me to be my best and committing your professional lives to improving our public school system. I am inspired by your decision.

To Keith, for staying the course, being true to yourself, and not quitting on me as a big brother.

To Paul Grinberg, my good friend. You will never know how much I miss you and value your opinion. I am eternally grateful for our nine years working together.

To Mike Barone, Uri Feldman, Chris Lee, Greg Koch, Dan Feder, Scott Huennekens, Drew Clark, Tom Garfinkel, Adam Boehler, Will Beamer, Jamie Levine, and Kelly Grismer, my good friends and YPO Forum mates. Thank you for always being there for me throughout my journey at Encore and for giving me the confidence that I could succeed.

To Carl Gregory and Barry Barkley, thank you for guiding a some-times-angry young man. I am honored to have worked with you.

To George Lund, for pushing me outside my comfort zone and making me a better CEO.

To Amy Anuk, for sharing your story, especially when it became uncomfortable. You're an amazing leader.

To Manu Rikhye, a once-in-a-lifetime talent. You taught me how to openly love your coworkers while holding them accountable to almost unattainably high standards.

To Greg Call, Jim Syran, Ashish Masih, Jay Cherry, and the other ridiculously talented executives I got to work with at Encore. This story doesn't do you justice.

To Fritz Heirich, for leaving a successful career to join Encore and for being a gentleman when it didn't work out.

To Nigel Morris, who took a chance on me at Capital One, taught me how to think, and was gracious enough to take my call many years after I left. You are a brilliant man with a huge heart.

To Shayne, who held the mirror in front of me and gave me a hug when I needed it. I look forward to our next collaboration!

To Lara Nuer, who knew exactly what to say when I was struggling and who cared enough to help me dig deep to connect to the emotions I suppressed for too long.

To G.W. Collins, my grandfather. I miss you very much.

Shayne Hughes

To Learning as Leadership's cofounders Claire Nuer and Sam Cohen, for creating the methodology we teach in our programs. In writing this book, I am simply a steward and a spokesperson for the practical insights you codified. (The methodology was later supplemented by Marc-André Olivier, Noah Nuer, Lara Nuer, and myself.)

To Lara Nuer, who co-led with me the leadership and culture change work LaL did with Encore. It's an injustice that none of the vignettes that helped convey the story described your invaluable part in Encore's transformation.

To Carole Levy and Marc-André Olivier, who coached many Encore executives and delivered WeLead to an ever-growing group of leaders within the organization.

To Jamie Babin, who played an important role in the early WeLead sessions and collaborated with Encore's HR team to enhance their impact on the organization.

To the entire LaL team, who helped make the writing of this book possible and who continue to bring this work to industries and organizations small and large.

To Jenny Jedeikin and Lari Bishop, who helped Brandon and me to make Encore's compelling story come alive on the page.

To Brandon, for your generosity of spirit, and for making our collaboration simple, inspiring, and ego free.

To all the employees at Encore Capital, who did the real work. My colleagues and I offer an opportunity for self-awareness, constructive communication, and clarity of purpose (and some nudging). You all took that opportunity and ran farther and faster than I believed possible

INDEX

competitive environment, emotional
safety and, 89

confirmation bias, 66

conflict avoidance, 60, 157

connection goals, 46

constructive communication, 122–130

  reactive, 128

  VEDEC, 127–130

Consumer Bill of Rights (Encore),
198–202, 207, 212–213

Consumer Credit Research Institute, 219

Consumer Financial Protection Bureau,
219, 222

context

  authenticity and, 197

  emotional safety and, 88

  noble goal and, 208, 217–218

  performance anxiety paradigm
  and, 216

contribution goals, 46

creative power, 140–149

cultural breakdowns, 75–82

cultural dysfunctions

  conflict avoidance, 60, 157

  defensive and guarded, 61

  healing, 121

  overwhelmed reaction, 61

  reactive behavior and, 57–63

  tactical reaction, 61

  Us vs. Them dynamics, 61

D

Deepwater Horizon, 216

default experience (self-fulfilling
prophecy), 68

defensive and guarded reactions, 61

"defensive ego", 137–138

derailers. *See also* cultural dysfunctions

  cultural, 61

  forms of, 35

  justifying, 12–13

desired and dreaded images

  Amy Anuk, 157

  overview, 17–18

  personality conflicts and, 65

  social side effects and, 62

  transparency and, 19–20, 62–63

direct communication, 129. *See also*
communication

diversity initiative (Encore), 170 171,
174, 208

downward spirals

  at organizational level, 72, 74

  personality conflicts and, 65

  reversing, 113–121

  self-fulfilling prophecies and, 67–69

dysfunctions

  healing, 121

  reactive behavior and, 57–63

    conflict avoidance, 60, 157

    defensive and guarded, 61

    overview, 57–60

    tactical and overwhelmed, 61

    Us vs. Them dynamics, 61

E

"ego is good" myth, 13

ego threats

acknowledging, 111

identifying, 55, 75, 119–120

knee-jerk reactions to, 38

pinches and, 52–54

recognizing, 20–29, 52

sharing, 128

value of defusing, 112, 174

egosystem

as cause of misunderstanding, alienation, and stalled progress, 156–159

characteristics of, 12

defined, 11

dollar cost of, 80–81

effect of underperformance on, 215

empathy and, 102

motivation, 73

recognizing triggers, 52–54

strengths and weakness and, 45–46

emotional clarity

behavior patterns and, 127

motivation and, 44–45

emotional safety

creating culture of, 100, 231

judgments and, 101

vulnerability and, 83–90

empathy

benefits of empathizing instead of judging, 197

egosystem and, 102

importance of combining with directness, 130, 172

during layoffs, 84

power of, 91–96

replacing judgment with, 120

VEDEC, 127–130, 146, 173

versus sympathy, 95

Encore Capital

changes in hiring, 113

Consumer Bill of Rights, 198–202, 207, 212–213

Consumer Yearbook, 209

developing transparency, 62–63

difficulties in 2007, 47

Encore India and, 75–80

finding noble goal, 198–202, 216–217

first seminar at LaL, 14–20

Investment Committee, 117–118

Investor Day, 183–187

managing layoffs, 83–104

"One Team, One Dream" initiative, 205–206

purpose of business, 3–4

second seminar at LaL, 32–38

2012 acquisition, 222–225

WeLead program, 59

Encore India, 47–48, 75–80, 96–99, 132, 203–204, 225

Enneking, Brian, 209

executives

feeling of powerlessness, 178–183

self-awareness of, 156

L

Learning as Leadership (LaL), 6–10

learning goals, 46

Levy, Carole, 161

listening skills

    constructive communication, 122–130

    reversing downward spirals, 113–121

    toxic habit of being right, 105–112

loops (self-fulfilling prophecies), 65–69, 74, 119

Lund, George, 114, 122, 133, 134–137, 139–149

M

Macadam, Steve, 138

"make others good", 145–149

"making others bad", 144–145, 148

Masih, Ashish, 191, 196, 198–199

mind chatter, 17, 53, 185, 231. *See also* desired and dreaded images

morale

    alignment between teams and, 113

    layoffs and, 96

    noble goal and, 209

motivation

    effect of behavioral patterns on life course, 159–166

    egosystem, 73

    emotional clarity and, 44–45

    fear of failure as, 215–216

    noble goal, 203–210

    power of commitment in face of failure, 210–219

N

noble goal, 203–210, 216–217

non-self-worth goals, 46

Nuer, Claire, 171–172, 198, 218

Nuer, Noah, 50–51

O

offensive ego, 131–139

Olivier, Marc-André, 94

"One Team, One Dream" initiative, 205–206

P

Peltz, Nelson, 2, 49

perception gap, 147, 170, 195

performance anxiety paradigm, 215–216

personal mastery, 121

personal responsibility, 183–190

personal value. *See also* desired and dreaded images

    personal success as measurement of, 215–216

    preoccupation with self-worth, 11

    putting aside preoccupation with, 197

perspective, reframing, 54

pinches

    biases and blind spots, 158

    defined, 52–53

    sorting, 53–55

ABOUT THE AUTHORS

———

Brandon Black

Brandon Black retired as the chief executive officer and director of Encore Capital Group in 2013. During his nine years as president and chief executive officer, the company built significant cost and operational advantages, expanded into new asset classes, and made acquisitions that established Encore as the industry's leading debt management and recovery solutions provider. In 2011, Encore started the Consumer Credit Research Institute, a groundbreaking effort to develop new knowledge about low- and moderate-income consumers using state-of-the-art research and fieldwork techniques. In addition, in 2013, the Great Places to Work Institute ranked Encore's subsidiary in Gurgaon, India, as the 14th best organization in the entire country.

Brandon earned an MBA from the University of Richmond and a

bachelor's of business administration degree from the College of William and Mary.

He is currently the president of the board for the Country Montessori School and the chairman of the board for Santa Fe Christian Schools. He also serves as a CASA (Court Appointed Special Advocate) for a foster youth.

Shayne Hughes

Shayne Hughes is president of Learning as Leadership, a culture change and leadership development firm serving the private and public sectors. His expertise in creating cultures of open communication and collaboration has led to substantial improvements in organizational and personal performance for such clients as Fairchild Semiconductor, NASA, Sandia National Laboratories, Shell Oil, and Capital One, among others. He is also experienced in the complex dynamics of family businesses.

Mr. Hughes has taught leadership at the University of Michigan's Executive MBA Program and the University of Virginia's Darden School of Business. He is a frequent keynote speaker at many conferences and corporate retreats.

Fluent in French, Mr. Hughes earned his B.A. from the University of California–Berkeley and completed graduate studies in group facilitation at the University of Tours in France. His writing has been published in Harvard's *Du Bois Review*, *Diversity Executive* magazine, Forbes.com, and *Chief Executive* magazine. He blogs for the *Huffington Post*.

Mr. Hughes also authored the coming-of-age memoir *When the Running Began*, in which he shares authentically how the pains of his past became infused with substance abuse and the coping strategies of his ego, and what it took to grow beyond them.